Flourishing in the Holistic Classroom

A volume in
Current Perspectives in Holistic Education
John P. Miller and Kelli Nigh, *Series Editors*

Flourishing in the Holistic Classroom

Lisa Marie Tucker
University of Winnipeg

INFORMATION AGE PUBLISHING, INC.
Charlotte, NC • www.infoagepub.com

Library of Congress Cataloging-in-Publication Data

A CIP record for this book is available from the Library of Congress
http://www.loc.gov

ISBN: 978-1-64802-546-4 (Paperback)
      978-1-64802-547-1 (Hardcover)
      978-1-64802-548-8 (E-Book)

*I dedicate this book to the memory of my parents
James and Carolyn Ilchyshyn, both extraordinary educators,
who cultivated my love of learning.*

Contents

Foreword xi
John (Jack) Miller

Preface xiii

Acknowledgments xxv

1   From Assembly Line to Nautilus Shell 1
    Flourishing in the Classroom 5
    Keen and Curious: Pedagogy 7

2   Dreams, Imagination, and Vision 13
    Dream Wisdom: If the Shoe Does Not Fit 13
    This Was a Sobering Thought 14
    A Vision for the Classroom 15
    Reimagining Education With Teacher Candidates 16
    Off the Assembly Line: Recalling the Self 20
    Holism: Reimagining Education's Framework 21
    The Way Forward: Holistic Curriculum 24
    Holistic Teachers and Schools 27
    Holistic Experiences for Teacher Candidates 27
    Author Note 29

3   The Heart of Community **31**

Planting Seeds: Eight Days of Community Building 31

Hospitality... 39

Deep Listening 41

Learning in a Holistic Context: The Findhorn Foundation
and Community.. 48

History and Founding Principles 49

Findhorn Foundation College... 51

Developing a Learning Community 51

The Gift of Inner Listening 55

4   Being Real: Paying Attention **59**

Pausing...Being...Contemplative Practice in the Classroom 60

Teacher Presence.. 69

Working With Fear: Being Vulnerable................................. 72

Challenging Behaviors... 73

Fear.. 74

Facing Our Fears 75

Dissipating Fear 78

5   The Seed.. **83**

The Inner Lives of Teachers and Students......................... 83

Holistic Curriculum 85

Quest for Wholeness: Spirituality in Preservice Teacher
Education 90

Spirituality and Religion... 91

Characteristics of Spirituality.. 93

Check Your Spirit at the Door: Spirituality in Postsecondary
Education 96

Spirituality in Teacher Education 97

Implications 99

Author Note 103

6   Voice and Choice: Inquiry-Based Learning **105**

Inquiry-Based Learning... 105

Peer Teaching 110

The Arts Camp 113

Initial Planning Sessions 114

Arts Camp Learning Objectives 115

The Arts Camp: What We Did 116

Teaching to the Spirit 123

Celebration of Learning 124

Feedback From the Students and Parents/Caregivers.................... 124

Implications 125

7 **My Journey**...**127**

Teachers' Experiences of Incorporating Holistic Principles
Into Their Practice 137

8 **The Invitation** **143**

References **153**

About the Author **159**

Foreword

In *Flourishing in the Holistic Classroom,* Lisa Tucker calls upon her years of experience as a teacher and teacher educator to address how we can truly teach holistically. This book is filled with examples drawn not only from her classroom, but also her experience teaching at a summer art camp and her time spent in the Findhorn community in Scotland. This book can inspire teachers to take risks to consider how they can work from a holistic perspective.

Lisa also includes many references from holistic educators such as Ron Miller, Sam Crowell, Rachael Kessler, Linda Lantieri, Ramon Gallegos Nava, Nel Noddings, and Parker Palmer so that her work is linked to significant scholarship in the field.

Lisa addresses the difficulty of teaching holistically in a time that is dominated by accountability measures that can stifle the teacher's creativity. Her book also explains how the spiritual needs of the student can be included in teaching in a manner that is inclusive and recognizes the student's inner life. I particularly liked the chapter "Voice and Choice: Inquiry-Based Learning" and how Lisa organizes her classes in a way that gives students opportunity to design their own learning experience including assessment. At first students were shocked as they never had the opportunity to engage in learning in this manner, but once underway the student involvement and excitement in learning was very evident.

The importance of teacher presence is emphasized throughout the book. Lisa includes a chapter on her own journey as well. She started as a public school teacher, then worked at a children's museum, and finally became a teacher educator. Lisa's presence is evident throughout the book; her commitment to holistic education comes through on every page.

—**John (Jack) Miller**

Preface

I invite you to recall a time in which you were engaged in a powerful learning experience. Perhaps, while reading a book you encountered a concept or an idea that you had not previously considered, and you began researching it in earnest. Or maybe a friend invited you to take an introductory skiing lesson with them, and you discovered that you had a natural aptitude for it and thus continued with lessons. As you recall the experience, identify what you were doing; where you were; who was with you; and the sounds, sights, and smells that accompanied it. Then recall if you had a mentor who guided your learning, as in the author of a book or a skiing instructor.

Finally, recall how you felt during the learning experience. Did you feel exhilarated, peaceful, happy, or challenged? Did time feel as though it was flying by, or did you feel as though you had been immersed in activity for hours and hours? We can all recall these powerful moments in which our inner world and life force engaged with an outer activity to create a memorable learning experience. We can also recall times of learning in school that were unbearable due to a lack of relevance in the content, less than optimal teaching methods, and a pace of teaching that did not necessarily match the pace at which we learned. Learning should not cause a student extended periods of pain or undue boredom, but rather, the learner should be engaged in the experience and feel a connection to what is being taught as often as possible. Learning is a natural dimension of being human, as without continually learning new things, we as a species would not survive.

Flourishing in the Holistic Classroom, pages xiii–xxiii
Copyright © 2021 by Information Age Publishing

Effective teachers consistently strive to create conditions that facilitate and support rich learning experiences for their students.

How then, do we assure that these rich learning experiences become a reality for as many of our students as possible? This of course, is our eternal quest; our *raisin d'être*, and I have spent well over 30 years exploring optimal ways to facilitate learning for students. In response to enquiries from colleagues, students, and workshop participants regarding how I create enlivening and rich learning environments for my students, I began to review and distill my years of experience to answer their question. I recognized that beyond theory, technique, and strategies that are commonly presented to preservice teachers, what really elevates teaching to a fine art are the principles, dispositions, and practices that we bring to our work that are less tangible, yet profound. These include teacher presence, hospitality, deep listening, and the capacity to be genuine and vulnerable with students.

Whether you are a parent, a teacher, a preservice teacher, a student, an educational assistant, a professor, or an administrator, this book is an offering to you of my experiences of introducing holistic principles into the institutions that I have worked in. Specific principles, dispositions, and practices that have become core components of my pedagogy are explored in detail. As teaching is a complex art, describing how to create a dynamic learning environment in which students flourish can sometimes best be accomplished using a narrative approach. Hence, this book weaves narratives with literature from key researchers in the field of holistic education. Many of the themes put forth in this book address our personhood as teachers, and although this is not often a focus in preservice teacher education, can make the difference between someone who knows how to teach and someone who embodies what a teacher truly is. The focus is more on who we are and how we teach, rather than what we teach.

The importance of developing community through hospitality, student voice, and deep listening, highlights how foundational this is to our work as educators. Introducing contemplative practice to students in the form of meditation and mindfulness, which has the potential to contribute to the development of an enriching learning community, is described. A discussion on teacher presence is included, describing how cultivating greater levels of awareness has a direct impact on everything that unfolds in the classroom. The aspects of fear and vulnerability, and how they influence a teacher's approach to classroom management, are discussed in detail, as many teachers find challenging behaviors of students to be one of the main reasons they leave the profession.

The centrality of creating an atmosphere in which students can engage their learning from the core of who they are is discussed, with numerous examples of how this can unfold. Harnessing and working with the interests of students is explored through the term "voice and choice," as inquiry-based learning is addressed using two examples from early and middle years contexts, and postsecondary education.

The teaching profession has become increasingly challenging for many reasons. The demands are great, curriculum is overburdened, student abilities and needs are diverse, levels of support can be inadequate, and greater levels of bureaucracy can feel oppressive. Due to these realities and others, according to Karsenti and Collin (2013), "In the United States, Reference (25) noted that the attrition rate is higher among teachers than in many other professions: 46% of new teachers leave their job in the first five years of service" (p. 143). There is minimal data available regarding teacher attrition in Canada.

The macrocosm to what unfolds in our individual contexts (and what influences the educational paradigm to a large extent) is a dominant North American society that can be described as extroverted in nature, competitive, fast paced, distracting, individualistic, bureaucratic, and imbalanced regarding distribution of wealth, resources, and power. In short, I would not characterize it as a healthy society or a place that is conducive to human flourishing. Greater numbers of people are realizing that some or most of their basic needs such as having a home, food, clean air and water, clothing, health care, education, and employment are becoming increasingly difficult to secure. The status quo is not adequate on most levels and many people are suffering.

We are experiencing a time of exponential change in many areas, including the advent of 3D printers that can manufacture cars and buildings, the technology to grow new organs for those requiring them, and artificial intelligence. Although many of these innovations are improving our quality of life, some of it has come at a great price, as Sanguin (2007) asserts, "The dissociation of science from ethics, and of economic interests from nature's limits, is literally killing us. The chemical soup we live in is a result of differentiation breaking down into dissociation" (p. 157). Sanguin adds, "Technology innovation is not a bad thing. The point is that when science and engineering are dissociated from spirit, morality, and ethics, the important questions don't get asked" (p. 157). We are destroying our home, the Earth through a focus on consumption and exponential growth at any cost.

The natural world is undergoing climate change at an unprecedented rate, with dramatic weather events occurring on a more regular basis throughout the world, causing hardship and displacement for many people. Berry (1999) describes that "the deepest cause of the present devastation is found in a mode of consciousness that has established a radical discontinuity between the human and other modes of being and the bestowal of all rights on the humans" (p. 4). We have forgotten our place in the cosmos through our disconnection to the Earth—our home and very source of our being.

In terms of economics, Pink (2005) asserts, "We are moving from an economy and a society built on the logical, linear, computerlike capabilities of the Information Age to an economy and a society built on the inventive, empathic, big-picture capabilities of what's rising in its place, the Conceptual Age" (p. 1). As this new age dawns, Pink claims,

> The defining skills of the previous era—the "left brain" capabilities that powered the Information Age—are necessary but no longer sufficient. And the capabilities we once disdained or thought frivolous—the "right-brain" qualities of inventiveness, empathy, joyfulness, and meaning—increasingly will determine who flourishes and who flounders. (p. 3)

These changes require us to balance the analytical left brain with the artistic, conceptual aspects of the right brain.

Zooming out and looking at the big picture, human evolution is also taking place whether we are cognizant of it or not. Beyond evolving from being hunter gatherers to organizing around agriculture, to the industrial, and then technological and information ages, more recently our species has moved through the specific generations of Baby Boomers, Xers, Millennials, Zers, and Boomets, each having their own characteristics and worldviews.

Since the late 1980s, there has been an emergence of more children being born with quite different aptitudes and characteristics, including being nonconformists, having a feeling of entitlement, possessing greater intuitive abilities, often having an over-excitable nervous system, and having an innate desire to make things happen to create positive change (Witts, 2009). A profound and recent example of the desire and action of these adolescents and young adults in creating positive change for themselves and others was their marches across the world demanding stricter gun control laws in the United States, in response to a mass shooting at a school in Florida. The teenage environmental activist Greta Thunberg has raised awareness around the globe regarding the climate crisis and has challenged policy makers and politicians to take action. These youth are not waiting for their parents or authority figures to address the crisis, but rather, are responding collectively to these situations by organizing and making their voices heard. Due to the characteristics and shift in worldview of these children, youth, and adults, their expectations of learning, working, and living are also different than those of their parents.

How then can people move beyond feeling overwhelmed, to responding to these changes and taking positive action in their lives? Perhaps in conversation with others who have a similar experience and concern, they form an action group or initiate a grassroots movement. Recently, in response to specific world events, people have begun to rise up and take action, and reclaim their power in many areas of their lives. Mass protests have occurred in Venezuela and Hong Kong in the last year as people took a stand against corrupt governments and despotic leaders. Many institutions are no longer viable, and people are responding by creating new models to address this, including communities who have their own currencies. This of course, requires great courage and running the risk of losing jobs, status, and the support of friends or family.

How can educators meet the needs of students in order to prepare them to live in a rapidly changing world? Positive changes in education are occurring in localized contexts as new models of education are explored and introduced. Educators are responding by initiating actions in their classrooms and schools that address specific issues that they face. If you work in an educational environment that is not positive or supportive, it is possible to create a positive learning environment in which you and your students will flourish. We have to move from an industrial, mechanistic form of education to one that is more organic, adaptive, and in alignment with the realities of the natural world.

Holistic education has much to offer educators in dealing with the challenges that they face in the current educational, social, and environmental climate, and to help them and their students to flourish. Principles that reflect the new educational paradigm include incorporating a variety of teaching approaches as identified by J. Miller (2010). These are the positions of transmission, transaction, and transformation. A focus on making connections in numerous ways including intuitive, body–mind, subject, community, Earth, and soul is another principle of holistic education that forms the fertile soil in which students can grow and flourish (J. Miller, 2010).

The organization of this book is based on the spiral; one of the most fundamental shapes in nature that reflects growth and transformation, and as Ward (2013) describes, "The spiral is the sign of the eternal, creative, unifying and organizing force or principle at work in the universe, and especially of the ongoing creation of consciousness" (p. 1).

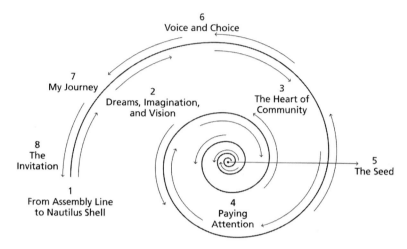

Figure P.1

Wesselman (2011) shares the wisdom of elder Hale Kealohalani Makua, "The spiral can remain static for a long time," Makua continued with a smile. "But it can change rapidly as energy flows into the spiral, or out of it. This is why we see the symbol of the spiral everywhere in the world of form in designs or in petroglyphs or pictographs in rock art. The spiral is the symbol for life" (p. 155). See Figure P.1.

This movement of growth and metamorphosis is an intrinsic part of how everything in the cosmos expresses itself. On a macro level, Ward (2013) notes,

> Our solar system came into being as a direct result of the spirality of our home galaxy, the Milky Way, and the arms of spiral galaxies are the birth-places of stars whose attendant planets are capable of seeing the evolution of life. (p. 108)

On the Earth, our home, the natural world expresses growth through the spiral movement of whirlpools, cyclones, and other weather patterns. Fern fronds and the seeds of a sunflower grow in a spiral movement, as does a chameleon's tail and a nautilus. We have a spiral in the cochlea of our ear, in our fingerprints, and in the fibers in the ventricles of our heart.

On a cellular level our DNA expresses itself through the double helix, which is based on the spiral, and Ward (2013) states,

It has been demonstrated that all forms of life grow according to the code contained in the DNA helix. It replicates cell construction, structuring the organism to resemble its parents perfectly with the inherited characteristics of both, handed down in the genes from the mother and father. (p. 125)

The spiral is a universal, ancient pattern found throughout the world and has been incorporated into human art, architecture, spirituality, and psychology. Petroglyphs, basket weaving designs, paintings, stones, and carved turf have been discovered with the spiral design. Ward (2013) describes, "At Skara Brae, the Neolithic 'Pompeii' of Orkney, a stone ball carved with a spiral ornament was found" and "Another Anasazi petroglyph, south of Albuquerque depicts the Morning Star god, next to a coiled snake in the form of a spiral" (pp. 33–37).

The golden ratio (Phi) or the Fibonacci sequence is found in spirals in nature. Ward (2013) states:

Specifically related to these spirals and to the Golden Section is the Fibonacci series, a mathematical progression introduced to Europe by Leonardo da Pisa (1170–1250), known as Fibonacci. Each part of the curve of the Pheidias spiral, for example, relates to the next in the series of proportion in which the last two integers of a sequence are added together to make the next number, for example: 1, 2, 3, 5, 8, 13, 21, 34, 55, 89, 144 and so on. The ratio of each term to the previous one gradually converges to a limit of about 1.618. (p. 57)

Sacred geometry arises from these observations of the natural world, describing the building blocks of the universe. It has been applied to numerous forms of architecture, and from the Greek Parthenon to the Giza Pyramids to modern civic buildings, the golden ratio has been employed.

When we consider the inner life of a person, the spiral is an archetypal symbol that has been used by humans for thousands of years to journey towards the divine. The basic movement is a circling to the center (to one's inner self or soul) and back out again on a single path. In ancient Crete a seven-circuit labyrinth was walked, and today the labyrinth in the Cathedral of Chartres is still walked by pilgrims. In Eastern religions the mandala served as a way for a person to symbolically journey to the divine, and as Ward (2013) notes, "The three circles, or planes, of spiritual evolution found in Druidic philosophy seem also to imply a spiral progression" (p. 11).

Ward (2018) describes:

The eminent Swiss psychologist Carl Jung said the upward spiraling of the kundalini serpent symbolized "the urge of realization (which) naturally pushes man on to be himself." For Jung, this involved the full realization of the Self, through the natural and universal process of individuation, by which a person is existentially formed and differentiated, and that he "saw the individuation process as a spiral progression."

The spiral then, as Ward (2013) defines it, is "a pattern of energy, itself made up of an infinite array of tiny spiral vortices—the spinning threads of sub-atomic particles themselves" (p. 114).

Pertaining to education, the spiral can be viewed as a movement between outer and inner knowing. If the outer edge of the spiral represents the outer or physical realm, as learners move along the spiral toward the center, they move toward the inner realm, which represents their true self or soul. In the outer realm, learners explore and experiment with concepts, processes, and skills development. In the inner realm they begin to reflect on their learning through contemplation, reflection, and in the process develop self-knowledge. They also begin to connect with their inner teacher or source of wisdom. In this model learners move along the spiral from the outside to the inside, and back out, continually, integrating inner and outer knowing. This spiral is not one dimensional, but rather moves outward into three or more dimensions.

In traditional education, learners experience an abundance of outer learning focused on activities and assignments designed to have them demonstrate their knowledge or skills base. Teachers use methods of transmission, with information being transmitted to the learners one way by the teacher, and transaction, with the teacher asking questions of the students, students asking questions, and students interacting with each other. Students go back and forth on the outer edge of the spiral and do not venture too far into the center. They do not have opportunities to reflect on their learning or have adequate time to integrate it with prior knowledge. With this focus on the acquisition of external knowledge, which is driven by curriculum, the inner life of the student is often ignored. How can learners create relevance if they have limited opportunities to connect to concepts personally?

An example of outer knowing would be learning about the life cycle of a frog by reading about frogs, looking at diagrams and watching videos of frogs, but never actually observing the process of a tadpole becoming a frog and logging the growth each day, recording observations, and reflecting on the process of metamorphosis, including what metamorphosis means to the students on a personal level.

When there is a balance between outer and inner knowing, students move beyond working with the physical realm and move deeper into the center of their being. As students learn, they have opportunities to reflect on their learning, generate more questions, and continue their inquiry. Meditation and other contemplative practices such as reflective writing facilitate students connecting with their inner life. Through these practices they begin to acquire self-knowledge and connect with their inner teacher. Using their questions posed through their reflection and contemplation, students then create relevance and meaning, and begin moving from the inside of the spiral into the outer realm, with purpose for their learning. This movement from outer ways of knowing to inner ways of knowing can contribute to transformation for the learner. Through the experiences that the learners have, in essence they walk the spiral towards deeper and more profound ways of understanding concepts, ideas, and themselves, and then integrate that knowledge into their external reality, as they begin moving out of the spiral.

In the organization of this book the movement begins on the outer edge of the spiral in the external world where we are physically situated; the Earth and the cosmos. The first chapter addresses who we are as organic beings living on the Earth and in the cosmos. It contains a description of my experience and perception of the current educational climate, having substantial remnants of the industrial era, which is counter to who we are and how we learn. The focus on consumerism is also addressed, including its impact on teachers and learners. I then offer an alternative and transformative paradigm that is more closely aligned to our true nature; holistic education.

Moving further along the spiral towards the center, Chapter 2 begins with chronicling a profound dream that I had many years ago that prompted me to begin writing this book. As the chapter title "Dreams, Imagination, and Vision" alludes to, a section of this chapter addresses changing educational paradigms through the example of an assignment that my students completed in which they were asked to develop a metaphor for teaching and learning.

The importance of developing a healthy community of learners is focused on in Chapter 3, including a description of the first eight classes in the course that I teach to preservice teachers. The creation of community is another step towards the center of the spiral, as it is fundamental for the development of the child, and key for all people who want to lead a fulfilling life. The role of hospitality and deep listening in the classroom are then described. This is followed by a description of my experience in the holistic learning center and ecovillage, the Findhorn Foundation and Community in northern Scotland, from which I have gleaned numerous approaches for fostering and maintaining a healthy community of learners.

Chapter 4 is an exploration of the role of mindfulness practice, which can facilitate a person's journey to their true self or soul, found in the center of the spiral in my model. This inner practice has the potential to transform us and thus inform our actions in the world. A detailed account of the process of introducing mindfulness practice to the students that I teach in a preservice teacher education program is focused on. The cultivation of the presence of the teacher is explored as well, particularly how mindfulness practice contributes to the development of one's presence, and subsequently, their actions in the classroom. This is followed by a discussion on fear and teacher vulnerability, and the importance of cultivating healthy relationships in the classroom.

The center or core of the spiral is reached in Chapter 5, with an exploration of the centrality of a person's inner world (their true self or soul) to their learning process. At the deepest level, the journey of learning is ultimately about a transformation that occurs within the learner, when externally formed concepts and ideas connect with the learner's inner world. The incorporation of the inner lives of students and teachers is the core of education that is often ignored but is essential to one's engagement in learning. The role of the spiritual dimension in the development of preservice teachers in particular is highlighted in a piece in which I summarize much of the research that I completed in my Master of Education degree. Although it is true that these inner practices are often ignored in education, many holistic educators have written about them, including Crowell and Reid-Marr, 2013; Lantieri, 2001; J. Miller, 2018; R. Miller, 2006; O'Reilley, 1998; and Schiller, 2014.

Beginning the movement from the center of the spiral back towards the outer world, Chapter 6 addresses inquiry-based learning, which is a key process that is often incorporated into holistic and transformative education. As a student or teacher chooses actions based on a connection to their inner world, they act from a place of freedom, responsibility, and purpose. Included is the experience that my husband Robert Tucker and I had facilitating an arts camp for children in the inner city, as well as an inquiry and peer teaching assignment that my students engage in.

As part of the movement from my inner self to the outer world of work, Chapter 7 describes the story of my journey as an educator from teaching in the early years, then directing programs and exhibits at a children's museum, to teaching in a faculty of education for the last 2 decades. These experiences in a variety of educational contexts provided me with opportunities to deepen my self-knowledge, which then informed my actions as an educator. It also contains commentaries by former students who now serve in a variety of capacities within the public education system, describing how being introduced to the holistic approaches in the courses that I taught them have contributed to their development and practice as educators.

The final chapter of the book ends on the outer edge of the spiral, where we reside on the Earth and in the cosmos. It includes an invitation to become more aware of our place in the grand universe, and of our role in sustaining life on our planet for all living beings through holistic educational practices. My hope is that you find inspiration in these words to reaffirm why you became a teacher, and to support you in your journey of incorporating a transformative educational paradigm into your classroom, and in the process, for you and your students to truly flourish.

Acknowledgments

The journey of writing this book has been one of joy, and I am fortunate to have had the support of many people throughout the process. First, I am forever grateful for the love and support of my husband Robert Tucker. Our collaboration at the University of Winnipeg over the course of a decade was rich and laid much of the foundation for this book. Since retiring from his position, our continued dialogue about education influenced many of the concepts and insights contained within these pages. He edited the initial manuscript and his contribution to Chapter 6 in particular was invaluable.

It has been a privilege to work with thousands of students during my career. I am grateful to have worked with students in the early years and to have witnessed their natural curiosity and interest in learning. I have been inspired by the enthusiasm and openness to exploring new ideas by the pre-service teachers that I have taught, and have been moved by their genuine desire and commitment to providing children and youth with rich learning experiences.

My gratitude goes to the University of Winnipeg's faculty of education for providing me with an opportunity to work with preservice teachers for over 2 decades in a variety of capacities.

I feel privileged to have worked with co-editors John P. Miller and Kelli Nigh. Jack reviewed my initial manuscript and provided me with guidance regarding the overall structure during key phases of my writing. Kelli's feedback prompted me to reflect more deeply on my work; in essence to

Flourishing in the Holistic Classroom, pages xxv–xxvi
Copyright © 2021 by Information Age Publishing

journey to the center of the spiral to my soul. This helped me to more fully paint a picture of how a holistic classroom supports student flourishing.

Many thanks to George Johnson of Information Age Publishing for publishing my work.

My deep appreciation goes to John (Jack) Miller, professor in the Department of Curriculum, Teaching, and Learning at the Ontario Institute for Studies in Education, University of Toronto, for writing the foreword to this book. He has been a mentor and trusted colleague for over a decade and has greatly inspired me through his scholarship.

In 2009, when I attended my first holistic education conference in Toronto, I was enlivened by meeting so many kindred educators. The connections that I made with colleagues and continue to nurture today have sustained me throughout this phase of my career. In particular, I am grateful to Gary Babiuk, senior scholar, faculty of education at the University of Manitoba, who has been a wonderful collaborator and mentor for many years. His feedback after reviewing the initial manuscript was a key contribution and our ongoing dialogue was instrumental in the refinement of the text. I am grateful to my friend and colleague Anne-Marie Collette, peace educator and intuitive life coach for women leaders, for her affirmation of my work. I continue to be inspired and supported by many other holistic educators whom I have met and worked with, as their pioneering work gives me hope that transformation in education is possible.

1

From Assembly Line to Nautilus Shell

The human is less a being on the earth or in the universe than a dimension of the earth and indeed of the universe itself. The shaping of our human mode of being depends on the support and guidance of this comprehensive order of things. We are an immediate concern of every other being in the universe. Ultimately our guidance on any significant issue must emerge from this comprehensive source.

—Berry (1988)

We are organic beings. Not only are we a part of the natural world; we are nature. Our bodies are made up of the elements of the universe and we are affected by the natural cycles and rhythms of the Earth and the cosmos. This chapter begins on the outer edge of the spiral in the physical world where we are situated. In this chapter I critique mainstream education which reflects the precepts of the industrial age, and then I provide an alternative model based on the principles and practices of holistic education.

For many people as they go about their daily lives including commuting to a city to work, being bound to technology, primarily working indoors,

Flourishing in the Holistic Classroom, pages 1–11

and seeing few trees, grass, or other flora or fauna, they gradually become divorced from the natural world—their home. Over time, this can lead to becoming disconnected from their very nature as well. Until quite recently in the history of our species, humans were inextricably connected to their immediate environments for reasons of survival, and they had a deep awareness of their role in the universal matrix. As Berry (1999) describes,

> That the human had such intimate rapport with the surrounding universe was possible only because the universe itself had a prior intimate rapport with the human as the maternal source from whence humans came into being and are sustained in existence. (p. 14)

Our ancestors had knowledge that had been passed down through generations to help guide them in all aspects of their lives from sourcing food to building shelter. The Polynesian people were able to navigate over thousands of miles using the wind, waves, sun, moon, stars, and migrating birds to guide them. We are part of an ecology that holds all life forms in a delicate balance.

As organic beings, children explore and learn about their world experientially using all of their senses. An example of this is a toddler at the seashore. They are fully present and do not simply observe the seashore, but rather engage it by walking in the sand and into the water, splashing the water with delight, feeling the shells, smelling the kelp, building castles with the sand and water, hearing the seagulls and the waves lapping onto the shore, and eating the sand. They are totally immersed in the environment of the seashore and experience it in a natural and holistic way. Time is not a concern for them, as they freely explore their surroundings. Until very recently in human history, children learned experientially in the context of their families and communities from people who had expertise in every facet of life. Learning was a natural part of everyday life rather than an activity that took place in a separate building with hundreds of students, dozens of teachers, and typically no family members.

Although we are organic beings, we continue to school children on an assembly line and give them components of information along the way, which reflects the industrial age some 250 years ago. When teaching is mechanical and technical, it is contrary to how the human brain actually works, learns, assimilates, retains, and retrieves information. Crowell and Reid-Marr (2013) describe that "by treating learning as mostly technical and linear, educators are in fact imposing mechanical solutions on open, adaptive, growing, developing, creative, meaning-seeking individuals. No wonder so many students are disaffected from the educational system!"

(p. 42). The teaching methods that may have been effective in producing people who would be compliant workers in factories, likely did not adequately meet most learners' needs then, and definitely does not suffice in the 21st century.

It is most unfortunate that we continue to support this form of schooling—one that is counter to who we are and how we learn—as these structures and processes that are imposed upon us force us to disconnect from our very nature. The Newtonian-Cartesian scientific paradigm negated previous knowledge and wisdom regarding the interconnected nature of the universe. Berry (1988) supports this:

> Our secular, rational, industrial society, with its amazing scientific insight and technological skills, has established the first radically anthropocentric society and has thereby broken the primary law of the universe, the law of the integrity of the universe, the law that every component member of the universe should be integral with every other member of the universe and that the primary norm of reality and of value is the universe community itself in its various forms of expression, especially as realized on the planet Earth. (p. 202)

Since the industrial revolution when people moved from rural environments to cities, the dominant school system could be described as train cars that are stuck on the rails. The cars are connected together in a linear fashion and are pulled along the rails by the engine until someone with the power to do so, disconnects and reconfigures them. Due to the manner in which the wheels rest on the rails, it takes great force to move the cars off of them. The changes that I am proposing in education are akin to the train cars being hoisted off of the rails and disconnected from the rest of the cars. The metal wheels would be replaced by self-driving wheels, which would then be free to move in organic, self-organizing ways just as true learning occurs. Learning would more closely resemble ivy growing up a tree, or fish swimming in a stream, than train cars on a track.

In most school systems throughout the world (predominantly public schools which provide free education for all), children are legally mandated to go to school and the curriculum is mandated by the educational authority of the government. In these systems the only part of the equation in which there is choice is on the part of teachers. Although teachers choose their profession, they are required to teach a mandated curriculum to students who are mandated to attend school. Depending on their context, there may also be expectations regarding how to teach the curriculum. Unlike most professionals, teachers are employees of the government, so must tow the line that the ministry of education mandates. For centuries, all participants in what we refer to as "schooling" have played their roles and tried to meet their expectations to the best of their abilities. Some fared well, while others suffered greatly. Today there are greater numbers of teachers, students, and parents who are calling for an educational process that supports and builds on learners' natural curiosity, that acknowledges their mind, body, and spirit and prepares them for living in a complex and interdependent world.

The current education paradigm in North America is also based on consumerism, that is, one's worth is determined largely by one's ability to produce or consume. Teachers feed students information, which they then consume. They often regurgitate the information in the form of a test or an assignment for the teacher to assess. This product-oriented form of education is not conducive to supporting learning or the overall well-being of all involved. It is externally focused, in that the product is revered, while process is often suspect. In many schools due to the overarching structure of the system, the inner lives of students and teachers are given minimal or no attention or support.

Universities and colleges have also become aligned with this system by becoming increasingly corporatized, and once students graduate, if they are not consuming or producing, they are often not valued as members of society. As the focus is on the external world, the inner life of the students is often viewed as not being valuable. An image that reflects this form of learning is that of a cat sitting on a windowsill looking outside; always projecting outward looking for stimulus but rarely venturing very far into the warmth of the home. As school systems attempt to meet the demands of commerce in creating learning objectives that prepare students for the workforce, other equally important skills, principles, dispositions, and knowledge are left by the wayside, such as developing compassion, self-reflection, flexibility, and the capacity for collaboration and risk-taking. John P. Miller (2018) speaks to this form of learning:

> This approach to learning is driven primarily by an economic agenda. We hear the mantra constantly that students need to be trained so that they can compete and participate in the global economy. This narrow vision of education has played a role in the corporate corruption that we see today. With the emphasis on individual achievement and test scores our system is basically one of student competition. Our students today are rarely given the larger vision of what it means to be human beings inhabiting the earth and the cosmos. (p. 96)

This dominant model contributes to the lack of engagement by many students at all levels of their schooling. From an early age, children who should naturally be playing indoors or outside with friends, are thrust onto the "hamster wheel" of schooling, never to get off of it unless they exert great courage in the face of pressure from all directions. They have no power, and when on occasion they exert it in the classroom, they are deemed unruly, and at times either put on Ritalin, a behavior modification program, or both. Rather than looking critically at how the organizational structure of the school system contributes to disenfranchising students, and committing to focusing on students and their learning, it is often easier to place the blame on the students, and to continue with the status quo, which is convenient for some of the adults involved.

The emphasis is on "producing" adults at the end of the assembly line who will be motivated to enter some form of postsecondary education or a trade, in order to secure a well-paying job that will enable them to purchase a plethora of material goods. We have replaced the education of students in preparation for them to become compliant factory workers creating products, with educating students in the hopes that they will become compliant consumers.

Flourishing in the Classroom

How then, can students be expected to connect with and integrate new learning if they are kept at arm's length by an overburdened curriculum, lack of time, and pressure to achieve? If education is about student learning, how do our current structures and practices support this? How can children's natural curiosity and love of learning be encouraged and supported rather than squashed? How can students and teachers flourish in their classrooms?

To flourish is much different than to survive. Flourishing is about going beyond basic survival needs; it means to be dynamic and growing. The innate inner impulse of the child is towards growth. In the classroom students flourish when they are allowed to be who they are and to express their ideas and opinions without fear of being harshly judged. They flourish when they are afforded choices in their learning whether that is through an option for an assignment or taking extra time to explore or experiment with a concept. Flourishing occurs when students are provided with opportunities and adequate time to connect with their inner self through reflection, and to incorporate their own ideas into their assignments, thus creating relevance. Students flourish when they are encouraged and supported by their teachers and peers, and where their learning is celebrated. This requires the teacher to create a safe and stimulating space in which students feel relaxed, happy, and have meaning and purpose in their learning. Seligman (2011) describes:

> Felicia Huppert and Timothy So of the University of Cambridge have de-fined and measured flourishing in each of twenty-three European Union Nations. Their definition of flourishing is in the spirit of well-being theory: to flourish, an individual must have all the "core features" below and three of the six "additional features." (p. 26)

In the chart the core features include positive emotions, engagement, in-terest, meaning, and purpose. Additional features include self-esteem, op-timism, resilience, vitality, self-determination, and positive relationships (Seligman, 2011).

Just as other living things on planet Earth require specific conditions in which to flourish, humans also need particular conditions if they are to flourish. In the context of our schools and classrooms this means creating an environment in which the students and the teachers can be the best version of themselves. Not only does this include cultivating the items on the previous list, but also by creating an environment that is relatively stress free, and where people trust and support each other. It is a place where tak-ing risks is supported, where people feel cared for, where expectations are clear and fair, where all participants have a voice, and where people can be their authentic selves.

Addressing the items on the list, we can ask ourselves if we display and model positive emotions for our students, and if our students are aware of what positive emotions are. I recall a teacher once telling me that he had to draw faces with happy and sad emotions on them and discuss them with his students, as they could not readily identify these basic emotions. I felt my heart sink as he was describing this, wondering how we had reached this point as a society. We can assess whether or not we provide learning expe-riences in which our students can develop an interest in and engage the concepts, skills, or processes. As we can all recall moments when a student asked us why they had to learn a particular concept or skill, it is important to be aware of the degree to which we provide students with opportunities to find meaning and purpose in their learning.

Addressing the six additional features, it is important to be aware of how we support students who do not have positive self-esteem to develop in that area. Reflecting on the degree to which we provide students with skills to develop optimism in their work is key. Do we model risk-taking to our students and support them in taking risks in their learning? As an essential life skill, it is important for us to determine if we model resiliency and support the development of it in our students when our efforts do not yield the results that we expect. Is there a sense of vitality in our being and is it cultivated in the group of students that we work with? Determining to what degree we provide our students with opportunities to make choices in their learning, including selecting or generating assignments is important if we want them to flourish. And finally, are the relationships between us and our students, and students and each other positive? Beyond the degree to which these features are present in our classrooms, does the school have an overall ethos that encourages and supports the flourishing of students and teachers?

In my spiral model, flourishing is a natural outgrowth of the fluid nature of moving from outer knowing to inner knowing and back to the outer on a continual basis. Each chapter outlines how the features of flourishing are cultivated by specific principles, dispositions, and practices inherent in the teacher's pedagogy. This movement is dynamic, as is human growth and the universe itself.

Keen and Curious: Pedagogy

In conversation with a colleague several years ago halfway through the fall term, she asked me how my students were doing, and I shared with her that they were keen and curious. She remarked that I consistently describe my students in that manner, and that it is the way in which I teach that allows me to view my students in such a positive light.

This exchange prompted me to closely examine my pedagogy. At this time I had taught teacher candidates in the third year of a 5-year Bachelor of Education program for over a decade. As I reflected on my pedagogy, what I soon recognized was that I have always taught in a holistic manner, and that student flourishing, whether in a public school classroom or in a higher education setting, has always been a priority for me. I am truly interested in students experiencing deep learning, not only about their subject matter, but about themselves as well. This interest in and concern for peoples' inner development has always been a part of who I am, and as a teacher I cannot determine how one can effectively teach students without addressing who they are on a deep level.

I am not alone in my efforts to teach in this manner. Holistic educators know that deep learning occurs when students engage their learning with the entirety of their being; their mind, body, and spirit (those being in no particular order). I understand that when students enter my classroom that they do not park their spirit in the hallway, but enter as whole human beings. If they are to experience deep learning and to flourish, they must be encouraged to engage their learning as whole people.

This of course requires teachers to be whole people as well, which in the workplace occurs best when administrators value this inner development and are committed to a process that facilitates and supports it. Finney and Thurgood Sagal (2017) address this issue:

> Seldom do teacher training courses, professional development offerings, or resources focus on the personal side of a teacher's development. Yet we found, and others confirmed, that personal development is the foundation of all other facets of professional growth. (p. xii)

Happy and fulfilled teachers are effective teachers, so a focus on the cultivation of the health and happiness of teachers must be a priority. As much of education in the western world is externally focused and students are processed on an assembly line, focusing attention on teachers' and students' inner lives is not given priority. This is tragic, as learning deepens when students are allowed to engage learning from their wholeness, and teachers also have a much more enlivening and gentle experience in the classroom. Palmer (1983) speaks to this, "Because conventional education neglects the inner reality of teacher and students for the sake of a reality 'out there,' the heart of the knowing self is never held up for inspection, never given a chance to be known" (p. 35).

There are many teachers who teach in a holistic manner. Unfortunately, the overall structure of most schools does not support this kind of teaching, as administrators are under pressure from policy makers to maintain standards (through preparing students for standardized tests), and to ramp up the pace. Highly skilled and experienced teachers often carry out their duties within an externally imposed structure that is more concerned with statistics and public opinion, than with the students and teachers for whom the system exists. The public education system was not created in order for administrators and policy makers to report on student test scores. It was created for the education of children and youth. What then, is an alternative to this system that is putting undue strain on all involved and causing suffering for many? How can we educate students to help them to flourish in their schooling and in their lives?

Holistic education provides an alternative approach to many of the issues that educators and students experience in the current educational paradigm. As Nava (2001) describes:

> According to the holistic vision, the universe is a living network of relationships, whose components are simultaneously whole and part. Human beings are one with this universe, and our consciousness is the consciousness of the universe. This new paradigm thus sees the natural world as a living world, which organizes itself in a manner that more closely approximates an organism than a machine. (p. 7)

Berry (1988) echoes this:

> We cannot discover ourselves without first discovering the universe, the earth, and the imperatives of our own being. Each of these has a creative power and a vision far beyond any rational thought or cultural creation of which we are capable. Nor should we think of these as isolated from our own individual being or from the human community. We have no existence except within the earth and within the universe. (p. 195)

Holistic education aims to educate a person by engaging their entirety, including their emotional, mental, physical, social, and spiritual dimensions. John P. Miller (2007) states that holistic education "attempts to bring education into alignment with the fundamental realities of nature. Nature at its core is interrelated and dynamic" (p. 3). This focus on interrelatedness and interconnectivity is at the core of holistic education. According to Schiller (2014):

> If we call ourselves holistic teachers, it means we have made a serious and lifelong commitment not just to our own self-development but also to philosophies that inform our practices, to the students entrusted to us, to the communities in which we work and live, and to the goal of changing our world for the better. It means we value creativity, sustainability, multiple ways of knowing, awakening the inner being in each of us, and living a life based on compassion, tenderness, love, and wisdom. Respect for all the faces of humankind is paramount as is the idea that people are transformed from the inside out. (p. 22)

If we are to create equilibrium in our education system and our world, and if we are to flourish, we must align ourselves with the fundamental realities of nature such as interconnectedness, and incorporate them into our teaching (J. Miller, 2007). We can no longer exploit our planet for our own purposes, but instead must elevate our level of consciousness, and thus develop a deeper understanding of our place in the natural world in order to regain a balance for all living things. It is incumbent upon educators to create the conditions in which students can flourish. In spite of the pressures to teach more curriculum, to assess student learning in a standardized method, and a plethora of demands placed on educators, it is possible to create an environment that focuses on learning that promotes student flourishing.

Developing a caring community where students feel safe to express their ideas and opinions, to ask for help, and to take risks in their learning without fear of being harshly judged through verbal feedback or marks is essential. Sharing power with students and encouraging them to make choices and direct their learning through inquiry-based learning leads to higher levels of interest and engagement by many students. As they have more of a personal stake in their learning, and discover relevance in their subject of study, students discover meaning and purpose in their learning.

The inclusion of the inner lives of the students is essential in this process, as they make greater connections to their learning and have a greater sense of agency. These are all holistic practices, which can transform teaching and learning by nurturing the inner life of students.

A holistic path encompasses key principles, dispositions, and practices that can contribute to an environment in which teachers and students are happily engaged in exploring ideas, concepts, processes, and skills together in an enlivened and relaxed manner. Even if your current education environment is less than ideal, hopefully some of the concepts and narratives in this book reflecting my experience of teaching children and adults, may resonate with you and inspire you to create a classroom that is enlivening, full of heart, and where you and your students don't merely survive, but flourish.

Flourishing is about feeling vital, engaged, safe, happy, and supported. Students do not thrive in environments that are competitive, and where they do not feel safe, cared for, supported, or are invited to engage their inner life in their learning. This chapter has offered a dynamic model of holistic education that cultivates students flourishing, including the core features and additional features of flourishing by Seligman (2011). The reality that numerous educators teach in a holistic manner was explored, emphasizing the fact that the structures that they teach in often do not support their work.

I am calling for an integral, holistic model that honors the abilities and experiences of educators and students, in an effort to make teaching and learning an experience of wonder and joy rather than a hardship. Higher levels of support in all areas must be refocused on the students and those who directly work with them on a daily basis. This will require the integration of dynamic, enlivening structures into the current structures. As human evolution is occurring (as we are experiencing during this time of a pandemic), educational structures must also change and adapt. Just as a chick breaks out of its shell that no longer supports its growth, so too must the outdated structures of education be broken through to allow new life to emerge and flourish.

2

Dreams, Imagination, and Vision

Your vision will be clearer only when you manage to see within your heart.
—Carl Jung (1958)

Moving along the outer edge of the spiral, this chapter focuses on a holistic educational paradigm and builds on an example of preservice teachers working with metaphors for teaching and learning. As dreams can provide us with powerful messages regarding issues that we are processing and perhaps struggling with, this chapter begins with a profound dream that contributed to my desire to write this book.

Dream Wisdom: If the Shoe Does Not Fit

In January of 2013, I had a vivid dream that spoke powerfully to me. In the dream I was teaching students in Grade 2, which was my favorite grade, and an administrator came to visit my class to speak with the children. The administrator was wearing a black Darth Vader mask and was speaking so quickly and in such an odd manner that I could not understand a word of what he said. It was as though another language was spoken. The administrator then indicated to me his desire to take the children outside, so I followed along at the back of the long line of skipping, singing children.

When we arrived outside, I noticed a climbing apparatus with materials for students to build structures, and when I asked the children where the man who led them outside was, they did not know. I was wearing a pair of slip-on summer shoes with backs on them, and as we waited for the administrator I noticed that my shoes were suddenly too small for me. I continued to try to fit my feet into the shoes but could not get the back of the shoe around my heel, as they were just too small. I tried over and over to fit into my shoes, which I had been wearing all along, to no avail. Each time I tried to pull the back of the shoe over my heel it didn't fit, so I finally had to fold it over and place my heel on top of it. After waiting for 15 or 20 minutes for the administrator to appear, I decided to lead the children back into the school. Once inside the school, I walked down several hallways trying to find my classroom and could not. At one point I passed by a classroom where the students were actively engaged in collaborative learning and some of their work was in the hallway, and it was so expressive and inspiring. I was envious of their stimulating and creative learning environment.

This dream profoundly affected me, and as I pondered it over the next few days, I began to realize that my shoes were indeed too small. Had my shoes become smaller or had my feet become bigger? Did the shoes represent the vehicle for my feet; my mode of transport in navigating the education world? As I reflected on this further, I realized that my feet had stayed the same size, but that my shoes had suddenly become smaller. I concluded that the shoes represented the institution of education; that the structure felt constraining to me; the shoes were metaphorically and literally squeezing me out.

This dream was an affirmation that my vision of education did not fit into the public school and postsecondary institutions that I had been involved in for nearly 30 years, and that I no longer fit in. In fact, I most likely never did fit in. My vision was much more expansive than the reality that I was working in. In the dream I kept trying to fit into the shoes, but could not, which mirrored my experience of trying diligently to work within an education system that I did not resonate with.

This Was a Sobering Thought

As I reflected further on my dream I began to wonder if my efforts towards helping preservice teachers to understand a more holistic perspective of education would really make a difference. Would helping them to connect to their inner lives affect them and subsequently the manner in which they would teach? Would I be able to bring heart into the academy to create balance and wholeness? How could I, with integrity, prepare my students to work within a system that I struggled to endorse? I contemplated these questions and more for several months. What happens when the shoe no longer fits?

I have strong opinions about the public education system, and during the last few years when my students asked my perspective on a variety of issues, I have had to somewhat temper my responses, (which became increasingly more difficult), as to not appear too biased or negative. I provided them with a wide spectrum of perspectives and encouraged them to critically examine and question all aspects of schooling, but if as Parker Palmer (1998b) states, "We teach who we are" (p. 1), I taught from wholeness and interconnectivity, so could not support a system that I deemed fragmented, competitive, consumeristic, and objectivist. I began to realize that my shoes were becoming too tight for my feet, and that the structure of the dominant educational paradigm was restrictive. The axiom "*one size fits all*" came to mind. One size does not fit all, or even most. I realized that I had a very different vision of education from the one that I had worked in for nearly 3 decades.

On a deep level this saddened me, as I had great hopes throughout my career that positive changes would occur that would focus on deep learning, a balance of inner and outer dimensions of students, offering the potential for transformative learning, with less emphasis on what teachers, administrators, and policy makers did, and with more emphasis on students and their learning. I had also invested a lot of my life energy working within these systems. With a sigh, I then began to purposefully review my career in order to gain perspective. Through this contemplation and in conversation with trusted colleagues, friends, and family members, several key themes emerged. These themes have been with me throughout my career regardless of what grade, subject, or whom I taught.

A Vision for the Classroom

Having a vision for one's life is crucial, including how it pertains to the work that we do. The vision that I have held for education has not wavered during my career, but rather has deepened and consolidated. An aspect that has been added to my vision is that I now believe that in order for a teacher's holistic pedagogy to fully unfold, they have to be in an educational environment that supports holistic practice on every level. Through the variety of experiences that I have had as an educator, I have always been keenly interested in teaching in an integral way. My focus has been on creating environments in which students could bring the entirety of who they are to their learning experiences. This requires an understanding and an acceptance that each student will learn at their own pace based on their particular abilities, learning styles, and interests, rather than trying to fit them into a predetermined system that is convenient for the teacher. Some students are able to adapt to and navigate the dominant education system with relative ease; that is, they conform by following the directions, doing the assignments in the manner prescribed, and receiving a reward for their effort. Many students do not naturally resonate with or buy into this system, and as a result suffer on a daily basis. They have difficulty finding relevance in their work and do not connect with much of the mandated curriculum.

Holistic educational practices offer much to these disenfranchised students, as they are invited and encouraged to connect who they are to their learning. One of the greatest gifts that holistic education offers learners is that their inner lives are acknowledged and honored, and they are encouraged to authentically explore and experiment with ideas, concepts, and processes. When describing one's vision and pedagogy, metaphors can serve as an effective way of doing so, as is explored in the following reflection.

Reimagining Education With Teacher Candidates

Mainstream education is an assembly line. This metaphor accurately describes the manner in which the majority of students in North America are schooled. This perspective is based on materialism, fragmentation, isolation of knowledge, and ultimately people. As the institution of education is a slow-moving machine, this metaphor does not reflect discoveries of frontier scientists, who now describe the universe in terms of interconnectivity, wholeness, and relationships.

My metaphor of learning as a spiral unfolds on a daily basis in my teaching, as I invite students to move from externally based knowledge and skills to their inner world, where they have an opportunity to reflect on their learning and integrate their inner thoughts and feelings into the subject that they are studying. The following assignment is an example of spiral learning.

Students taking a course that I teach that focuses on teaching and learning, in the Bachelor of Education program at an urban university in Western Canada, gave me much to consider as I marked their final assignment 8 years ago. The assignment required the students to develop a comprehensive framework of their understanding of teaching and learning. They were to include a description of

1. their teaching philosophy,
2. how to create a community of learners,
3. teaching methods and strategies that they would employ in a specific context,
4. the five most important teaching qualities deemed by them,
5. where classroom management resided in their model,
6. an image or visual representation of their model, and
7. I also encouraged them to use alternative modes of representation to support their written work.

Although not required in the assignment, I was intrigued that almost every student used a metaphor for teaching and learning. A metaphor is a figure of speech that uses a phrase or a term and applies it to something that it does not literally apply to, but rather resembles. J. Miller (2007) notes,

> Another tool for enhancing intuition is metaphor. Metaphorical thinking involves making connections between two words or ideas that are not normally related, but which share some commonality. For example, the human kidney is like a fuel filter in that both screen out certain molecules. (p. 102)

The use of metaphor allows students to make connections between one object and another while drawing on their imaginative and intuitive capacities.

The metaphors for teaching and learning that my students developed included a city, the human heart, a soccer team, a car, the ripple caused by tossing a pebble into water, and a bridge. Another metaphor was a papier-mâché tree, with the roots and trunk representing their teaching philosophy, the branches representing the development of community, teaching methods and strategies, teaching qualities, classroom management, and the leaves representing the growth and uniqueness of each student. One student developed their metaphor for teaching and learning as if learning can be likened to a candle being lit. He described the soul of the learner as the wick, which is the core of the candle. The learner soaks up knowledge and experiences, just as the wick absorbs the wax and moves it upward. The student relies on their learning environment to foment learning, as the surrounding wax is the fuel that the wick pulls up and ignites. Learners require a solid foundation in order to learn knowledge and skills, like candles that have to be placed in a container in order to be stable and safe. The teacher ignites the students' interest and curiosity, just as a flame is required to light a candle. At times a teacher has to try several approaches in order for students to learn a concept, much like a match that may have to be struck several times before it bursts into flame.

These were powerful examples of the depth of understanding that these students were developing for the complex and dynamic art of teaching. Their clear and imaginative articulation of these concepts demonstrated their capacity to make connections. J. Miller (2007) supports the use of metaphor in holistic education, "Metaphorical teaching asks students to explore connections and make intuitive leaps" (p. 103). Based on the quality of work that the students submitted, they demonstrated how readily they were able to make deep and meaningful connections between their subject of study and who they were as preservice teachers.

Klein (2010) recognized the power of metaphor in students' multimedia journals, stating that

> it is clear from the wide range of responses and metaphors that students overall believe that teaching involves attending to the whole person/student and that teaching involves the body (physical presence), mind (knowledge) and spirit (capacity to inspire and dream). (p. 51)

These findings supported what I was observing in my students' assignments, as they reflected on the learner as a whole person.

What struck me was the manner in which most of the students articulated the principles of holistic education and expressed a desire to incorporate them into their teaching practice. Initially, I wondered if this was predominantly due to my holistic pedagogy (theory and practice of teaching), even though I only dedicate a few classes to explaining holistic teaching and learning explicitly. Were the students representing these concepts in order to appease me and attain a higher grade? This may have been partially true for a few students, although the depth of our classroom discussions and their willingness to challenge ideas and the status quo did not support this assumption. I then began to wonder if perhaps my holistic pedagogy was giving them permission to tap into something deep within them that they strongly resonated with. Perhaps they were remembering what true learning was, and subsequently giving themselves permission to create a safe space within which to reimagine the possibilities that holistic education may hold for them in their careers as teachers. The metaphors that they created illustrated the degree to which they had made deep connections with their inner self or soul.

Most of these students have experienced 15 or more years of schooling, complete with outcomes-based curricula, standardized testing, individuation, reductionism, competition, and a focus on preparing them for the workforce as productive citizens. Ron Miller (2001) describes the results of this focus,

> Our considerable powers of intellect have served primarily to disconnect us from the world. Modern systems of education have fed these powers well, training young people how to gain knowledge *over* the world, knowledge at the expense of feeling, information without wisdom, facts without moral discernment. (p. 31)

If this mechanistic method of educating students was in fact effective, and contributed to students not only developing the capacity to solve problems, analyze concepts, be flexible, collaborate with others, and exercise their imaginations, but also contributed to their levels of happiness, fulfillment, and self-actualization, then I would not be writing this book. And if teachers were professionally challenged, affirmed, happy, fulfilled, and healthy, then I would also confirm the success of these methods. Kohn (2011) states that "if a certain approach to teaching left most of *us* bored and unenlightened, we probably shouldn't teach another generation the same way" (p. 5).

From a critical perspective, teachers and students are to some degree, the unwilling participants in a life-draining drama akin to the *I Love Lucy* television episode in which she and her coworker could not keep up with wrapping the chocolates due to the speed at which they were coming down the conveyor belt. They were under threat of losing their jobs if they did not perform, were under time constraints, had a demanding boss who did not allow them any freedom, resulting in tremendous pressure. They were doomed to fail from the start, and at one point, Lucy stated that they were fighting a losing game. The scene ended poignantly with their boss asking the controller of the conveyor belt to speed it up.

Although a comedy, this particular scene echoes drama and pathos. This drama unfolds in classrooms on a daily basis as teachers feel pressed to not only teach the prescribed curriculum (particularly if they have standardized tests to prepare their students for), but are pressured by their administration to adopt new programs, and at times perform their duties without adequate support. Similar to Lucy and her coworker, teachers are engaged in quality control of the students that they process.

The implications of current partitioned and reductionistic curricula are that they inculcate a worldview for children that is not natural to them, as they innately view and experience life more holistically. Children can experience discomfort, and at times, suffering when they are taught in a manner that focuses on partitioned facts and disconnection, when their intuitive and experiential understanding of how things work stems from a position of connection.

Rather than students being herded from class to class with buzzers and bells, following the carrot at the end of their noses in the guise of grades, holistic practices invite the learner to explore concepts and skills in an experiential manner, and to engage the exploration from the core of who they are.

Off the Assembly Line: Recalling the Self

In this assignment my students expressed an interest in and an understanding of holistic education. During our time together over two semesters I focused on helping them to unpack their schooling, education, and field experience in a critical manner through activities and discussions. Looking critically at one's conditioning can be simultaneously challenging and illuminating. We engaged in sharing, discussion, viewing movie clips, viewing art, having guest speakers, reading, writing, group work, and student presentations. One of the main threads that was woven throughout these experiences was their observations of students in the schools in which they had their practicum, who were often disconnected, unmotivated to learn, unhappy, and angry. As we collectively unpacked these observations, attempting to get at what was really happening, I realized that the challenging experiences they had in their practicum placements, often stemming from inappropriate student behaviors, provided rich material for remembering what true learning was.

Perhaps my students began to remember what true learning felt like when they engaged in the final assignment. I provided them with clear criteria regarding the content of their assignment, however, I invited them to use multiple modes of representation. Besides the papier-mâché tree, a graphic novel, a model of the human heart, a book, a board game, a painting, and a series of letters were submitted. Through varied modes of representation, each of these assignments revealed not only essential understandings of teaching and learning, but an authentic representation of the human who created them. It was evident that my students were making powerful and personally meaningful connections. Rather than teaching and learning being an assembly line, based on the dominant institution's metaphor, these preservice teachers were connecting with their own metaphors. The inner and outer realms were integrated in powerful ways, and as holistic education is based on the principle of teaching to the whole person, these creations exemplified this interconnectivity and wholeness. As Nava (2001) states,

> Holistic education is not indoctrination within the existing culture; it is not training to compete with or control other human beings; it is not merely a process to reproduce society's existing conditions. It is an act of transformation. It creates the pedagogical conditions for an unfolding of the unlimited inner potential of every student. (p. 44)

Through the invitation to engage mind, body, and spirit in their representations of their models of teaching and learning, perhaps my students were given permission to begin remembering not only their learning in its multiple forms, but themselves as well. In a paper about spirituality in teacher education (Tucker, 2010), I wrote,

> If one engages the "real" world by being disconnected from self, perhaps that is what one ultimately comes to know: that learning is fragmented and that since the learner is not in relation to the subject, the learner ultimately does not matter. (p. 5)

The work of remembering oneself takes time, support, and a safe environment, as most students have spent 12 or more years being metaphorically dismembered on the assembly line called school.

Holism: Reimagining Education's Framework

What then are the possibilities for reimagining an education that would also encompass the inner lives of students and teachers? What new metaphors for teaching and learning could be cocreated by those involved in education? These are not new questions. In fact, educators and philosophers including Jiddu Krishnamurti, Maria Montessori, Rudolph Steiner, and A. S. Neill were prompted to develop educational models that were a response to the pressing issues of their times, and that provided viable alternatives to the status quo. Today, Montessori and Waldorf schools are among some of the fastest growing holistic schools in the world.

Montessori education is based on hands-on learning experiences that reflects constructivism and was not only informed by the work of Maria Montessori's contemporaries such as Vygotsky and Piaget, but also by her interest in the areas of peace and inclusion. Maria Montessori, who was a physician with a specialty in psychiatry, developed a daycare program for preschool children in a neighborhood in Rome (Dorer et al., 2019). Her theory of planes of development was based on four distinct development planes that each lasted 6 years from birth to age 24. Dorer et al. (2019) share:

There are many guiding concepts of Montessori pedagogy, but they can be briefly summarized by Dorer's (2017) statement of ten core principles, which are respect, creativity, freedom of movement, freedom of choice, freedom to repeat, the prepared environment, the planes of development, mixed age groups, independence, and holism. To bring each of these principles together in the classroom environment, Dorer (2017) states that the catalyst of Montessori education is the Montessori teacher who directs the classroom and activities within it. (p. 163)

Montessori education is a clear example of holistic education, as the focus is on the whole child and on introducing children to whole concepts before individual components. She called this cosmic education, and as Dorer et al. (2019) describe,

The purpose of Cosmic Education is to help the child understand the unity of the universe: acknowledge the long path of universal history that has led to the present, recognize their own role within not only that history but also the evolution of the earth. Through such a macro-experience, Montessori envisioned learning that is naturally enchanting and inviting. (p. 163)

I am not proposing a departure from intellectual ends, but I am suggesting that we need to restore a balance between inner and outer ways of knowing in which the inner life of the student is encouraged to engage with the outer barrage of facts and figures. As I previously wrote (Tucker, 2010), "As knowledge becomes a commodity which one wields in the world rather than something that one comes to deeply know and love, it ultimately breeds dispassion" (p. 6), and the adage that "knowledge is power" makes one wonder what kind of power that ultimately is, whom the power resides with, and how is it used. Holistic education offers an enlivening approach to teaching and learning by creating learning environments in which students have opportunities to more fully engage their learning.

In the context of postsecondary education, the introduction of holistic pedagogy is a risky endeavor, as the entire system is structured on fragmentation, positivism, and defending of positions. The rigors of academia also demand that our subject be studied at arm's length rather than us being in relationship with it. As Palmer (1998b) asserts:

Objectivism, driven by fear, keeps us from forging relationships with the things of the world. Its modus operandi is simple: when we distance ourselves from something, it becomes an object; when it becomes an object, it no longer has life; when it is lifeless, it cannot touch or transform us, so our knowledge of the thing remains pure. (p. 52)

Hence, subjective knowing becomes unreliable and suspect. As postsecondary institutions increasingly adopt corporate models, the aims of holistic education are frequently ignored, and subsequently, those who teach holistically are often excluded from essential decision-making processes. Those for whom teaching and learning is a forest or a symphony, must carry out their jobs within a dominant metaphor more akin to teaching and learning as a competition or a sales transaction.

It is time for standardized learning to be replaced by a holistic approach that more aptly reflects new scientific understandings that confirm what mystics and metaphysicians have always known; one that acknowledges the interconnectedness of everything in the universe and that focuses on the wholeness of the learner (mind, body, and spirit). Education as an assembly line reflects the Newtonian paradigm, and as McTaggart (2008) describes,

> The world as machine, man as survival machine—have led to a technological mastery of the universe, but little real knowledge of any central importance to us. On a spiritual and metaphysical level, they have led to the most desperate and brutal sense of isolation. (p. xxv)

This paradigm may have proved efficient for administrators and policy makers in pumping their product out, and some of them may even boast about their school being a "well-oiled machine," but one has to wonder how effective and life affirming the experience has been for both students and teachers.

Focusing on a holistic, integrated approach, J. Miller (2007) describes three principles of holistic education including balance, inclusion, and connection:

> The focus of holistic education is on relationships: the relationship between linear thinking and intuition, the relationship between mind and body, the relationships among various domains of knowledge, the relationship between the individual and community, the relationship to the earth, and our relationship to our souls. (p. 13)

This focus on relationships naturally extends to the creation of a connected curriculum, in which relationships between concepts, ideas, disciplines, and the students are at the core of learning. R. Miller (2006) asserts:

> One could argue that Western culture and education have been dominated by the yang, which tends to emphasize the rational, the material, the masculine, and the individual to the exclusion of the intuitive, the spiritual, the feminine, and the group. This imbalance, one could argue, has led to sickness in cultures and institutions. (p. 7)

Change is occurring, albeit slowly, and as Nava (2001) points out,

> Over the past ten years, a holistic vision of our realities has been taking shape in the fields of ecology, biology, and physics. The knowledge being developed in these new sciences is overcoming the materialist myths to which society has clung for the past three hundred years. (p. 6)

The balance of inner and outer worlds has the potential to reorient us to what being truly human is, and to subsequently reenergize a tired, overburdened education system.

How then, can we stop the assembly line and assist students in remembering what true learning is? I offer three ways forward. First, holistic teaching and learning begins with whole teachers. Second, educational leaders must acknowledge and support holistic principles. Third, preservice teacher education programs must respond to the call from students, teachers, and parents alike for a new way forward, by offering preservice teachers holistic educational experiences.

The Way Forward: Holistic Curriculum

When I ask my students to describe an influential teacher, they do not list the use of wait time or organizational skills as the main characteristics of these teachers. Instead, they describe human qualities, such as being present, caring about the students, and being passionate about their subject. The assembly line can be stopped, and holistic education can gain ground as teachers consciously become whole, thus embodying and modelling wholeness to students through their presence. J. Miller (2010) echoes this, "I believe that more than anything students want our full, authentic presence, and through this presence the teacher connects with the students" (p. 97). Beyond methods and techniques, teacher presence has the most powerful impact on students and their learning. Being mindful and present in the classroom can be cultivated through establishing a commitment to any number of contemplative practices such as meditation, yoga, tai chi, or walking. Teacher presence develops through sustained focus on the inner life of the person, and from the support of others as they engage in this inner exploration and self-development. As institutional change is a slow-moving machine, unlike Lucy's chocolate conveyor belt, teachers can cultivate holistic learning in their classrooms as they themselves become whole. This requires time for them to personally remember themselves and the establishment of communities of practice to support them in this important work.

As teachers remember themselves, relationships with their students deepen, and subsequently, the learning community deepens as well. I have written previously about spirituality in education, and after completing a review of the literature, determined,

> What is important to note is that most of the characteristics of spirituality identified in this paper are relational, and that the teacher must facilitate ways for students to enter into relationships and interrelationships with their subjects, their peers, themselves, and the world. (Tucker, 2010, p. 8)

What is currently externally imposed and highly valued can be balanced by the inner worlds of teachers and students also being honored.

The majority of holistic educators create a plan for an integrated curriculum and then allow the dynamic of the class to inform the learning experience. It is a balance of thoughtful planning, paying attention to where the student interests and abilities lie, and trusting that the path that the teacher and students are forging will lead to rich learning experiences.

Through remembering our wholeness, we awaken from our amnesia, and are able to see the wholeness of the universe. Everything in the universe is interconnected and whole; it is we who have created separations that do not exist. We have been under the illusion that we are separate. As R. Miller (2006) states, "If we experience interconnectedness and interdependence, a natural sense of compassion for all beings tends to arise. Not seeing ourselves as separate, we feel a basic connection to living beings, both human and non-human" (p. 19). We have an opportunity to move away from a fragmented curriculum that largely serves the needs of policy makers, administrators, and society through training individuals for the workplace, to an integrated curriculum that meets the needs of the whole person, creating meaningful learning and existence. Imagine the possibilities that this approach could hold for the planet and all beings who inhabit it.

Teachers who draw from holistic principles incorporate particular teaching approaches that draw the learners into deep learning, and education becomes less about the teacher and focuses more on the learning of the students. In order to reach a student's mind, body, and spirit, a wide range of teaching approaches and strategies must be drawn from. J. Miller (2007) describes three teaching approaches or orientations: transmission, transaction, and transformation. The transmission orientation focuses on the teacher transmitting ideas and concepts to the students, who then receive them. J. Miller (2007) states, "Knowledge is seen as fixed rather than as a process, and is usually broken down into smaller units so that students can master the material" (p. 10). There are times when using the position of transmission is the most appropriate for the concept or skill that you are teaching. In my classroom, I use transmission when I want to outline a specific process or address key concepts initially in a lesson. When you are preparing to take off in an airplane, the most time efficient way of explaining the safety regulations is for the flight attendant to quickly demonstrate while giving directions. Imagine the chaos that would ensue if the flight attendant led a discussion or question and answer instead.

The transaction position most commonly involves dialogue between the teacher and the students and as J. Miller (2007) describes, "In transaction learning, the student must often solve a problem or pursue some form of inquiry. Knowledge is not viewed as something that is fixed in small units but as something that can change and be manipulated" (p. 11). I have my students working in cooperative learning groups on a regular basis to solve problems or work on case studies regarding specific teaching and learning situations, and I consistently observe an increase in their levels of engagement.

The last position of transformation works with the child as a whole person, and "the student is not reduced to a set of learning competencies or thinking skills but is seen as a whole being" (J. Miller, 2007, p. 11). Described in greater detail in another chapter, I invite my students to engage in a listening activity with a partner and then in triads. They take turns listening to each other without interrupting, asking questions, or giving advice to the speaker. This proves to be a powerful experience for my students, as they begin to realize the degree to which they listen to others.

Incorporating these teaching approaches helps to foster a climate of respectful, engaged learning. Rather than singling out one approach as being dominant, teachers balance the approaches, incorporating the ones that most readily facilitate specific kinds of learning. This requires preservice teachers to have knowledge and experience of the positions of transmission, transaction, and transformation, in order to have a breadth of teaching approaches to draw from. As students begin to explore ideas and concepts in a deep way and as they have more voice and choice, they begin to remember what true learning is. This in turn, motivates them to further their inquiries into their subject areas. As Nava (2001) notes:

> The holistic educator has a radically different view of the student. The student is not seen as a brain to be programmed, but as a human being with unlimited inner potential, a sensitive being oriented toward learning, a spiritual being capable of recognizing life's inherent beauty, who embodies the multiple dimensions of the human experience. (p. 44)

Holistic Teachers and Schools

To facilitate holistic learning in the classroom, leaders must support teachers in this endeavor through visionary thinking, the backing of solid research, and trust in teachers to teach and students to learn. This will occur as leaders observe educators teaching holistically and witnessing how enlivened and engaged their students are. They may then begin an inquiry into holistic education either through dialogue with teachers (and spending time in their classrooms) and/or through reading literature and attending professional development opportunities. Administrators must be willing to go out on a limb and challenge the status quo regarding standardized testing and the negative impact that this practice has on teachers and students, as the assembly line is largely driven by standardized testing and the accountability movement. The characteristics of servant leadership have the potential to support this shift, as servant leaders support teachers in doing their jobs to their fullest potential by serving first and then leading. Rather than imposing structures on teachers, this style of leadership focuses on supporting and trusting teachers.

Exemplifying a new paradigm, Robert Greenleaf (2003) who created the term *servant leader* in the 1970s, said that "the servant leader is one who is a servant first" (p. 16). The ten characteristics of a servant leader are the ability to listen, have empathy, the ability to heal, awareness, persuasiveness, the ability to conceptualize, having foresight, having a commitment to the growth of people, and having the ability to build community. It is incumbent upon the leadership to provide resources, time, and support to teachers who ultimately have the greatest impact on students. Teachers must also be trusted to assess student learning and development in a manner that is congruent with holistic approaches, rather than being mandated to use assessment strategies and tools that do not reflect holistic philosophy. As the public education system exists for the education of children and youth, the focus must shift from creating and sustaining policies, to supporting students and those who work directly with them.

Holistic Experiences for Teacher Candidates

In order for the assembly line drama of education to be replaced by a more integrative, holistic approach, the realization that the current corporate, materialistic, and mechanistic approach to education is not contributing to the well-being of teachers and students must be acknowledged. If we continue to educate students with fragmented bits of knowledge in courses, which themselves are fragmented from larger bodies of knowledge, how then are we preparing them for thinking and working in an interdependent world? This means, of course, that the political agenda that prevails must change, and that a focus on the greater good of all must come before the building up and defending of personal and collective egos and agendas.

Preservice teacher education programs have the greatest potential to provide teachers with holistic learning experiences and knowledge. One must experience holistic principles in context, to fully appreciate and understand them, before incorporating them into one's teaching. This can most fully be realized through embodied teaching, as the modelling of this approach is essential to the depth of understanding it. J. Miller teaches graduate courses in holistic and contemplative education and spirituality in education at the Ontario Institute for Studies in Education in Toronto, Canada. The University of Hawaii at Hilo's School of Education is one of few postsecondary institutions to offer a preservice teacher education program with a holistic focus. Their mission statement reads:

> The UH Hilo Education Department is dedicated to the holistic development of transformational educators who are committed to equity, empowerment, and a critical understanding of our world. The Department envisions its future as the heart of a learning community of caring, ethical, and creative people as faculty seek to fulfill the following mission: to promote the professionalization of teaching by providing and engaging in educational experiences that are holistic, empathic, artistic, rigorous, and transformational. (University of Hawaii, Hilo, 2019)

Greene and Younghee (2019) support the inclusion of holistic pedagogy in preservice teacher education:

> There is a critical need to embrace the significant role for personal development in a holistic pedagogy of teacher education. To do so is to acknowledge that we teach—first and foremost—from within. Through a pedagogy of self-development, course curriculum is framed around the centrality of the whole *person* relative to theory, subject knowledge, and skills. This approach invokes the emotional and spiritual nature of who we are as whole human beings. (p. 100)

In public education, The Equinox Holistic Alternative School, which opened in 2009 in Toronto, Canada, offers hope for holistic learning in their mission statement,

> At Equinox, we strive to build a solid foundation for learning that will successfully carry our students forward, not only through to Grade 8, but beyond. Our students are encouraged to become thoughtful, productive, and caring Canadians who are environmental stewards within their local com-

munities, and avid life-long learners. (Equinox Holistic Alternative School Parent Council, 2021)

Nava (2001) also addresses the need for education that addresses key issues in society by stating,

> We need a new education that nurtures and is consistent with the new emerging culture. In this new society, holistic education recognizes the tremendous importance of educating for global citizenry and planetary awareness, that is to say, the importance of educating for interdependence. (p. 116)

Forest schools throughout the world provide students with opportunities to learn in the context of the natural world, and they have been growing by leaps and bounds over the last decade.

These schools and preservice teacher education programs are powerful examples of holistic education, amidst the dominant paradigm dictating that the assembly line speed up. I got off of the assembly line a long time ago and have no desire to hop on again. Based on the responses of my students in our discussions, most of them are not on it willingly either. I am grateful to my students for inspiring me through their insightful and powerful metaphors, and through their thoughtful and mindful participation in dialogue in our classroom. They have provided me with renewed hope that we do not have to be willing participants in the assembly line called school, but with integrity can choose to jump off of it and allow a more humane and life-giving metaphor of education to emerge.

If teachers are to embody and teach from wholeness, and if students are to engage in the process of discovery and real learning, we must move to teaching and learning as a tree, a bridge, or the human heart. Students and teachers must be afforded the time, leisure, freedom, and lack of pressure in order for a reimagining of education to truly occur.

Author Note

The preceding writing is based on an article that was first published in the nonextant journal *Encounter: Education for Meaning and Social Justice*, Volume 25, Number 2 (Summer 2012).

3

The Heart of Community

One sees clearly only with the heart. Anything essential is invisible to the eyes.
—*The Little Prince*
by Antoine De Saint-Exupéry (1943)

Planting Seeds: Eight Days of Community Building

All humans have an innate desire to belong, whether to a family, a sports team, or a workplace. We are social beings who require interaction with others to help define us, support us, and to collaborate with on a variety of daily tasks, sometimes for our very survival. In the classroom real learning cannot occur until the community has begun the process of developing. This chapter moves further along the outer edge of the spiral toward the center, as the interactions that occur within the community of learners provides individuals with experiences that contribute to their self-knowledge; in essence people become a mirror for each other regarding who they are and how their ideas and behaviors impact others. The three key components of community development that are focused on are cooperative and collaborative learning, hospitality, and deep listening. These components

Flourishing in the Holistic Classroom, pages 31–58

cultivate one of the core features of flourishing, which is positive emotions, as well as the additional feature of positive relationships.

When I taught young children in the early years of my career, I spent the entire month of September on community development including creating a safe space for learning to occur, developing trust, and teaching the students how to work cooperatively. I taught them what each particular role in a group was, such as the facilitator or recorder, and supported them as they learned how to take on each role. I also focused on teaching them how to listen to each other and to cooperate in their work together, whether at centers or in table groups. This was my vision regarding how my students would work together as a community, and it was well worth the time, energy, and careful planning. A few colleagues inquired as to why I was spending so much time on this, as there was so much curriculum to cover. I never regretted doing so, as the emphasis on community development made teaching and learning much easier in the long run. As the students acclimatized to their new environment, to new peers, and to me, they began to feel comfortable asking me or their peers for help, expressing themselves, and taking risks in their learning.

I model this for the preservice teachers that I work with, as I want them to have an experiential understanding of the importance of how to create community. I devote eight classes at the beginning of the 26-week course (78 classes), specifically, to community development with my students. Humans cannot learn deeply if they feel isolated, have minimal support, are stressed out, or are under pressure. The development of a stress-free environment in which students feel that it is safe to express themselves, to ask questions, to challenge the status quo, and to take risks is one of the most essential aspects of any learning environment. Crowell and Reid-Marr (2013) address the results of a classroom that does not meet these needs,

> Emotional distress can also come from impersonal or depersonalized classrooms, a lack of community, a sense of not belonging, or seemingly irrelevant content that does not speak to students' interests or needs but nevertheless has high expectations or conversely very little expectation that some students can succeed. (p. 116)

It is our responsibility to create fertile learning environments in which students have all of the necessary nutrients that they need in order to flourish. According to Noddings (2003), "The atmosphere of classrooms should reflect the universal desire for happiness. There should be a minimum of pain (and none deliberately inflicted), many opportunities for pleasure, and overt recognition of the connection between the development of desirable dispositions and happiness" (p. 246). The development of a positive learning community has to begin to take root before learning can occur. This is even reflected in the scientific world as cellular biologist Lipton (2005) describes a mentor speaking about cloning stem cells, "He told me that when the cultured cells you are studying are ailing, you look first to the cell's environment, not the cell itself, for the cause" (p. 19).

The teacher education course that I teach focuses on the practical skills of teaching and learning, including lesson and unit planning, classroom management, assessment, classroom design, and an array of teaching strategies. The following is a summary of the first eight classes of the year that I purposefully designed to facilitate the development of community.

Day 1

I have music playing that sets a relaxed, yet stimulating tone, and I greet students individually as they enter the classroom. Once students have found a seat, are settled, and I welcome them to the class, I ask them to recall a teacher who was influential in their education and to write down the characteristics of that teacher that made them memorable. Through this recollection, they connect with the essence of a master teacher in a multisensory manner. I then ask them to create groups of four, which means that they will meet at least three new people within the first 10 minutes of the class. After introducing themselves, the group members then take turns sharing the characteristics of the teacher that they recalled and then record them on chart paper. The chart papers are posted on the whiteboard, at which point I invite the students to get out of their seats and stand around them. There is a feeling of curiosity and anticipation as I overhear students asking their peers why they have to leave the safety of their tables. At this point the air is electric and there is a quality of immediacy, as my students interact with their work and that of their peers. As they gather around their first piece of work as a community, I feel very present as I observe their engagement and the expressions on their faces. It is a deep collective experience. I ask them to look for commonalities among all of their lists and they do this with great ease on a consistent basis. As the commonalities are identified, I tell them that these are some of the qualities or dispositions that we hope to cultivate in ourselves during the course of the year.

What I have gleaned from student feedback is that this activity is important in setting the stage for learning due to the fact that they are collaborating with peers right away and they are asked to be reflective as they recall an influential teacher. For many of them, there has been a particular teacher who supported and encouraged them on their path to becoming a teacher. They then bring their work together as a collective and their ideas are the first thing they encounter in the course, rather than a course outline. This act of soliciting and honoring their voices is both simple and profound.

This is then followed by another activity, which prepares them for the next class in which I introduce holistic pedagogy. Students remain in their groups and each is given a bag with random objects such as a paper clip, a small globe, a rock, a letter "L," and perhaps a small toy animal. Each bag contains a different assortment of objects. I ask them to take the objects out of the bag and place them in the center of the table. Their task is to find as many connections between the objects as possible. Once the students have determined as many connections as possible, I ask each group to briefly share their results with the rest of the class. Typically, they discover that they each have a unique way of making connections, with some groups creating a narrative using the objects, and others sorting them according to identified characteristics. I then speak briefly about one of the main principles of holistic education, which is connection.

Finally, before leaving the classroom, I ask students to fill out a recipe card with information about themselves to help me to get to know them better. This includes their major subject, minor subject, experiences they have had related to teaching, their career aspiration, and anything else they deem important in helping me to support their learning. Rather than my students filling out a form digitally and submitting it online, I ask them to give me a physical card when they leave and to introduce themselves to me, in order to make a physical connection. I believe that this first greeting sets a tone of hospitality. Students report that they enjoy working with others in a group on an engaging activity, and when they leave the classroom at the end of the initial class, they are typically very enthused, and are talking to people in their group about the class. This initial class is designed to facilitate interpersonal connections between students and to encourage them to begin thinking about the importance of connection. Mission accomplished.

Day 2

An expectation at the university is for instructors to go over the course outline within the first few days of the semester, so that is the first item on Day 2. I then do a presentation on holistic education in order for students to begin to understand my pedagogy, as it is quite different from that of mainstream educators. The main principles of holistic education as articulated by J. Miller (2007) are balance, inclusion, and connection. In alignment with holistic practice, I inform them that the pace at the beginning of the course is intentionally slower than they may experience in most classes, to give us time to begin the process of building relationships within community.

Day 3

Is It Lunchtime Yet?

As many educators can attest to, games are an effective way to begin to develop community, so Day 3 begins with the students and me playing several games. The first game is a warm-up, and is pretty low key, as to not intimidate anyone. We move all of the furniture to the periphery of the room, and they simply walk around the room (I do as well) and approach a peer and say two things. The first is their name and the second is their favorite food. This is a loud activity as 30–36 people are milling about and chatting, but once they get into it the students seem to enjoy it. The atmosphere is quite festive and is akin to being at a party or other social event, meeting new people, and at the end of it they have met everyone in the class.

Knowing Me, Knowing You

I usually vary the second game, but one example is Smarties. I discovered this game a few years ago as one of my students did his inquiry and peer teaching assignment on ice breakers. He did several ice breakers with his small group and gave them each a brochure with a description of each activity. In groups of four or five, I give my students a bag of Smarties and a sheet with a code on it. One at a time, each group member selects a Smartie and depending on the color they select, they have to answer a question on the code sheet. If a student selected a green Smartie he or she would answer the question: "Where would you love to live for a year?" Food is usually a motivator for students, so this game works very well. This exercise allows them to get to know simple things about their group members, and they usually discover that they have something in common with one or more of their peers.

Developing Agreements

The second half of the class is dedicated to creating expectations or agreements for working as a community. The first purpose of this exercise is for the students to determine how they are going to work together during the course of the year. The second purpose is for me to model one way of developing guidelines or agreements with a class, as they will begin their practicum experience in schools the following week and I want them to be observant of how the guidelines or rules are developed in their particular classroom. Students sit in small groups of four or five and have to come up with expectations that they have for the course, the instructor, and their peers. I then ask for their ideas in each category and write them on the whiteboard. Once all of their ideas are on the board, I then address each item and use it as an opportunity to let them know what my approach is. An example is if the students have an expectation that the instructor will give feedback in a timely fashion, I let them know the timeframe in which I typically return assignments. Another expectation that students often include is that they would like to work with each other in a nonjudgmental manner. On one occasion, a group's expectation of the instructor was to bring cookies to class! Of course, I followed through and baked cookies, which I took to their class at the end of the semester.

This process allows the students to specify exactly what they expect of the course, their peers, and me, and has proven to be a powerful exercise in that they have voice throughout all of the activities and have made a clear commitment to their guidelines for working together throughout the year. Their expectations are fairly standard from year to year, including doing one's fair share of the work in a group and being supportive of each other, but as noted, there are a few interesting variations at times, such as wanting me to take cookies to class.

Day 4

Questions

Rather than immediately plunging in with my agenda, I devote the fifth class to the questions that the students have about education. In inquiry-based teaching and learning, identifying specific questions that students have about a topic is part of the initial phase. As we have already reviewed the course outline and the students have a better sense of the trajectory of the course, I feel that it is important for them to have input so that I have a better sense of what their interests and key questions regarding education are. I ask the students to ponder what their biggest question is about education and I give them adequate time to contemplate this. I then ask them to write their question on a colored recipe card. When they are finished, the students then tape their cards onto pieces of chart paper on the front whiteboard.

When all of the cards have been attached to the chart paper we then begin to look for common questions and themes and then group them together. The key questions remain on the chart paper and we leave these on the wall for the duration of the course and review them at times throughout the course and at the end. This becomes a visual reminder of key concerns of the group, and as we address each question during the course of the year, they come to understand that their questions are valued. I have observed that students are quite surprised that their questions are not only solicited, but honored. This exercise deepens the community experience and the connections between people.

Day 5

One of the assignments that happens six times during the six-credit hour course is a coop discussion based on a relevant topic related to teaching and learning. Students are placed in groups of five to seven members at the beginning of the year. Prior to their discussion all of the students read four or five articles and watch a video pertaining to the topic. Two sample articles are "Social Networking Addiction: Emerging Themes and Issues" (Griffith, 2013) and "Have Smartphones Destroyed a Generation?" (Twenge, 2017). They then meet and have a discussion, led by one of the group members, who then takes the information from the discussion and melds it with the research from the articles and writes a short report.

Zooley

In order to prepare them to do cooperative work, students engage in a cooperative learning activity. An example is Zooley, which is a cooperative exercise based on deductive reasoning and symbolic thinking. Each group is given a map of a zoo that uses a different language. Rather than having pictures of animals, there are symbols or shapes such as circles or triangles representing animals in particular groupings. An assortment of patterns such as wavy lines or dots is used for each group of animals and the sizes and numbers of animals also vary. There is a list of questions about each group of animals and the students have to work together to determine which symbols represent which animals. One group member is also tasked with observing the process that the group used to solve Zooley.

Through my observations, most students find this to be quite a difficult exercise at first, but once a leader emerges to get them started, and they answer a few questions, they are able to identify which symbols represent particular groups of animals. Once all of the groups have solved the puzzle, the group members who also observed their process share the specific strategies that their group used to solve Zooley. Some students thrive on solving Zooley, while others have challenges completing it, which I believe is due to their lack of experience with problem-solving, and divergent and symbolic thinking. This sets them up for working on a specific task or issue as a group, which they do the following week in the first coop discussion.

Day 6

Mindfulness

The last day of the initial phase of community development entailed students engaging in a co-op discussion on media, technology, and screen time. In short, I decided to introduce mindfulness practice to my students many years ago in response to an overwhelming number of them talking to me about their struggles with anxiety and depression. My intention was to offer a practice that had the potential to ease suffering for my students and to assist with inner transformation. It took deliberate planning regarding how to introduce this practice and I based most of the exercises on my experience of practicing meditation and mindfulness for over 2 decades. This practice has proven to be a key contributor to the development of a healthy learning community and is thoroughly addressed in detail in Chapter 6.

Day 7

During the last 5 or 6 years, I have observed that students are increasingly distracted by their phones and laptops. After reviewing current research on the impact of social media on people and students in particular, I decided to address it right at the beginning of the year. I begin the class by showing a TED Talk by Sherry Turkle called "Connected but Alone?" (Turkle, 2012, 19:48). It is an excellent talk in which Sherry describes her work as a researcher 15 years ago touting the advantages of cellphones and social media. She now shares her current research, which indicates that although people feel that they are more connected to others, they are actually more alone.

After the TED Talk, I facilitate a whole class discussion on the way in which we use technology in our lives. It is usually a very illuminating discussion and students are often candid in their sharing. I then request that when they are in my class, that they do not have their phones on their desks unless they are expecting an important call or text message. I let them know that in order to have our full attention on what we are learning, the phones are nothing more than a distraction. I request that they keep their phones in their bags unless they are expecting an important call or message. Most students respect my stance and refrain from having their phones on their desks, and they are usually engaged enough in class to not have time to check them. I have discovered that having this candid discussion based on current research has a positive effect on the classroom tone, as all participants have an opportunity to voice their opinions and experiences. This class prepares them for their first co-op discussion on the topic of media, technology and screen time.

Day 8

Co-op discussion on media, technology, and screen time. All of the students read articles and watch a video pertaining to this topic, followed by a discussion in which one group member facilitates, takes notes, and incorporates key points from the discussion, the readings, and their experience as a student and preservice teacher in a paper. The specific statement is: Given the increasing presence and pressure for technology and computer literacy to be included in classrooms and schools, a growing body of research examines the potential repercussions of increased media, technology, and screen time (MeTS) for children and adolescents. Using the co-op readings and your experience as preservice teachers, defend or refute the role of MeTS within students' lives with regards to social development, physical well-being, and academic performance.

By the end of the first eight classes my students have had opportunities to interact with each other in a variety of capacities, and as a community have laid the groundwork for our year together. Kessler (2000), who wrote extensively on soul in education, describes the importance of developing community in her work with young people:

> After the groundwork is laid, students begin to find the comfort or the courage to begin talking about their own lives. Personal storytelling brings a group to life because it ensures that students speak about what they have experienced and know. It gives speakers a sense of authority over their own lives and begins to develop the listener's capacity for empathy. Through their stories, students reveal what in their lives awakens and feeds their soul. (p. 8)

Some agreements have been reached regarding how we will work together, and important discussions have been initiated, in which all voices have been solicited. It usually takes another few weeks of sitting in silence together at the beginning of each class for a sense of unity to take root. I have found that this approach to community building has contributed to an enlivened and peaceful learning environment for all involved.

Hospitality

My husband has taught me the art of hospitality. Until I entered into a relationship with him, I was unaware that I was not as hospitable as I could be to visitors in our home. This was revealed to me one evening when I suggested that it was time for our guests to go home, as I was quite tired. What I have learned from him is that hospitality is the key to developing healthy relationships and community. It does not mean that you have to spend a lot of money on providing your guests with food and drink. What it does mean is that you greet people warmly when they arrive, offer them food and beverages, and make sure that they are comfortable. It is about being welcoming and giving them care and attention. This translates to the classroom as well, as it is essential that students not only feel welcome in our classrooms, but that they are invited to make it their own during the course of the year.

There are many ways in which we can offer hospitality to our students, including greeting them when they enter our classroom, making sure that no one is left out of a group during discussions, and making ourselves available to them when they require assistance. Several years in a row, as students entered the classroom on the first day, I approached them, introduced myself, and shook their hand. They appeared to appreciate the fact that I had noticed and greeted them. I have also discovered that simply smiling at students has a tremendous impact on them, especially if they are not feeling their best. A simple, genuine greeting at the beginning of the class can make people feel welcomed. On particular days when I sense that their energy levels are rather low, I take an energy check by asking them who has a level five (being a lot of energy), four, three, two, and one. This provides me with important information regarding how to proceed with my agenda and if many students are quite depleted of energy, I might lead them through a guided visualization to help them to recharge their energy or ask them if they would like to do a small or large group discussion.

For a period of 3 years I taught in the basement of an old building; a bus depot to be exact. It looked like a regular classroom with whiteboards, a projector and screen, tables and chairs, except that it had no windows, two air ducts in the ceiling that would roar throughout most of each of my classes, and the smell of sewage and cigarette smoke wafted into the space on occasion. I found it difficult to hear my students and had to over teach, resulting in me losing my voice several times one term. It felt like being in the bowels of a ship.

In the winter semester of the first year that I taught in that space, I observed my students flagging during an afternoon class. I spontaneously suggested that we have a Café on Fridays to help boost our energy. This caught their attention, and within seconds they offered excellent suggestions regarding what we would need, and I recorded them on the board. The next week we instituted Café Fridays. I bought some kettles, tea, hot chocolate, instant coffee, and each cooperative learning group took a turn bringing in treats each week. As the weeks progressed, I began to realize what a positive impact this was having on the students and their enthusiasm for learning, particularly on Friday mornings when the temperature was –30°C. The groups started bringing in interesting assortments of treats and became quite creative in their offerings, including one group who brought in fondue.

Palmer (1998b) speaks of the importance of hospitality in the classroom, "Good teaching is an act of hospitality toward the young, and hospitality is always an act that benefits the host even more than the guest" and adds,

> By offering hospitality, one participates in the endless reweaving of a social fabric on which all can depend—thus the gift of sustenance for the guest becomes a gift of hope for the host. It is that way in teaching as well: the teacher's hospitality to the student results in a world more hospitable to the teacher. (p. 50)

It was evident that this simple act of hospitality was having a positive effect on my students, and that they looked forward to it. I also benefited from the more festive atmosphere, as my students were happier and more eager to learn. Beyond greeting students as they enter our classroom and assisting them as needed, there are many ways in which we can extend hospitality to our students.

Deep Listening

Humans have a need to be acknowledged and accepted, and one way to experience this is by being genuinely listened to. Regardless of the size of the class that you teach or the context, it is possible to create community through active and deep listening. One of the fundamental practices that I have used throughout my teaching is providing students with opportunities to share their ideas and opinions, and to be truly heard without fear of being judged. This demonstrates to the students that the teacher genuinely values them and I have recognized that deep listening is fundamental to building relationships and creating a dynamic learning community.

We often do not really listen to others. Many of us have had experiences of attending a meeting and listening to colleagues' ideas regarding the issue at hand. Perhaps we heard their words, but rather than fully listening to them, we were rehearsing our response. In the Western world this is a habitual way of relating to others that begins early in our socialization. In an educational context due to many students vying for attention from one teacher, or people at a meeting who are dealing with a heavy agenda and time constraints, this pattern can become a norm.

When a person seeks counsel with either a trusted friend or a professional, what they seek more than anything is to be heard. They don't necessarily want advice or to be fixed. What they truly seek is for someone to just listen to their story without interruption; a witness. This seems to be so simple, yet for most of us, it can be difficult to achieve. Most of us have been socialized to talk a lot and to fill all of the air space with words. We are often inundated by a constant stream of chit chat from television programs, commercials, the radio, and places of work. In some situations, people have to almost fight their way into a conversation to have their voice heard.

O'Reilley (1998) describes the barriers involved in learning to truly listen to another:

> Don't all of us know how to listen? On the contrary, I think we know how to shut down. Self-preservation compels it. Modern life—with its din of Muzak and commercial entreaty, its appeals and drives, its reviews and performance evaluations—trains us not to attend but to tune out. There is much to hear, but little worth listening to. In an environment of overstimulation, the commitment to spend time, simply listening, constitutes a radical experiment in friendship. (p. 17)

Classrooms are places where having "dead space" can feel awkward, and teachers can feel pressured to talk 80% of the time or more. This is an expectation created by socialization in schools, which is a reflection of a culture that is dominantly extroverted. It is also a reflection of a dominant European cultural influence, as many other cultures do not communicate in such a verbose manner.

My husband shared an experience with me that he had regarding listening, when he took the Rolling Stock Museum into Northern Manitoba in the 1970s. He worked for the Manitoba Museum (at the time it was called The Museum of Man and Nature) and designed a railcar with museum exhibits that he installed in it. The theme of the exhibits was the Fur Trade Society specifically between The Pas and Churchill, Manitoba. Most of the railcar encompassed the exhibits, and a small living space took up the remainder of the car. The railcar was then hitched up to a train and the journey up north began. The car was unhitched on the siding of all communities between The Pas and Churchill for residents to visit for varying periods of time. During this time he enjoyed his interactions with the people in each community, and had many experiences of Indigenous people in these communities coming to explore the railcar. Many of them sat quietly beside him for some time, waiting until they felt that they were on the same energy level. They were attuning to each other. Then a few words or a gesture from either party would validate what they were communicating. He readily eased into this way of being and communicating with people, and by the time he returned home, it felt natural.

Upon his arrival home he attended his first meeting with the staff of the museum in the boardroom. There he sat quietly with his long braids and wearing a buckskin jacket. As he had become accustomed, he sat quietly and waited for everyone to feel that their energies were in sync before speaking. At some point he heard fingers tapping loudly on the table. He looked up and the head of the human history department suggested that perhaps he was not ready for the meeting and recommended that he go home and rest. My husband's colleagues were prepared to ask him questions, expecting him to share his experiences with the museum on wheels, so displayed discomfort at his silence. In relaying this story to me, my husband commented that he felt perfectly fine; it was his colleagues who needed to go home and rest. It is important to recognize that not all of our students will come from cultures as verbose as our dominant culture and they may feel disoriented and not at ease in our classrooms.

This urge to speak constantly may also partially arise from the belief on the part of the teacher that if they talk, the students won't have opportunities to talk and become unruly. This allows the teacher to feel in control of the learning environment as they are directing the interaction. As teachers are typically the main adult working with 20–40 students, they may also feel pressure to over talk in an attempt to keep everyone engaged.

In my experience when students have regular opportunities to discuss ideas and concepts with their peers, they actually stay more focused and engaged in their learning. Over a decade ago in response to budget cuts, I was asked by the administration to teach two classes of over 100 students each in a lecture hall. I could not imagine teaching that many students but looked at it as a challenge and a learning opportunity, so agreed to teach one of the two sections. I spent the summer doing research on teaching large classes and put a plan in place. Two teaching assistants were allocated to me, which made a positive difference for me and the students. As I designed the course, I recalled once being a student in those unwieldy lecture halls, with some of my peers sitting in the nosebleed section either falling asleep or cramming for an exam. That of course, was back in the mists of time prior to the advent of computers and laptops, so today many students play games or shop online while sitting in the "rafters."

My plan included a balance of lecture and group work in order to keep students engaged. During each class, they had at least 10 minutes to talk to their neighbor about an issue or concept, and sometimes 10–20 minutes to discuss a teaching and learning scenario or a specific topic with three other people sitting beside them. The teaching assistants moved through the lecture hall, as I did, answering questions as needed, and students became quite adept at assuming yoga positions as they turned around in their seats, which were fixed to the floor. I found this method highly successful, as most students were engaged throughout each class. Of course, some of them found it quite odd that they would not be able to doze off 10 minutes into class as they anticipated that I would lecture nonstop, but they soon adapted to this method. I succeeded in creating a dynamic community within that large class.

The development of a positive community cannot occur if very few people take up all of the talk time and others' voices are rarely heard. If we desire to build healthy, democratic learning communities, we must create spaces in which all voices have an equal say, and we must also learn how to truly listen to others.

Listening to our students is essential, as it enables us to learn more about who they are, how they learn, and what their gifts and challenges are. Schoem, Modey, and St. John (2017) support this,

> More deeply, many students hope that their teacher, in advancing their learning about content and theory, will also take an authentic interest in them as vibrant, complex, individuals and in who they are; what they think and value; and what their challenges, hopes, beliefs, and dreams are. (p. 80)

This reflects the qualities of memorable teachers that my students identified at the beginning of the year.

My preferred mode of teaching is a balance of introducing concepts and providing my students with experiences that allow them to further explore the concepts. After I share information with my students in class or after they read an article or a chapter from a book, I often take them through an activity. I then help them to unpack their experience, including insights or challenges that they had, as well as how they might implement the specific process or strategy into their teaching, or modify it to fit a specific context.

Every year I engage my students in a listening exercise to create greater awareness of how they listen to others. This occurs in the second semester of the year when students know each other well and a level of trust has been established within the group. The first part of the exercise consists of people working with a partner. I provide them with a topic, and each person has 3 minutes to talk about it. An example is: "What is the most interesting thing you have done in the last 2 months?" One person responds to the question and the other person listens. The person who listens cannot interrupt, ask questions, give advice, or add to their comments. Their only job is to listen.

The second part of the exercise consists of groups of three people working together. Each person has 3 minutes to speak on a given topic, and the other two people listen to them. An example of a question is: "What are you most passionate about?" After the first person speaks, the other two people take a moment of silence, and on a small piece of paper, they write a probing question for the speaker that will help them to further explore what they spoke about on a deeper level. The questions must be open-ended to facilitate such an exploration. The same process is then followed by the other two group members.

At the end of both parts of the exercise I facilitate a discussion on the process and encourage people to share their experiences. Some people feel uncomfortable being the speaker and having one or two people listening to them, without having an opportunity to respond or interact with them. Others find it very positive, as they may not have regular opportunities in which they can speak and have the full attention of others without being interrupted. Some people who are in the role of the listener have a difficult time not being able to respond, interject, or ask questions. Others enjoy having the pressure taken off of them, by just being the listener. The discussion then focuses on how teachers listen to students, how students listen to teachers, and how students listen to each other.

This exercise appears somewhat simple yet is always quite a profound experience for my students, as they gain a new level of awareness regarding how they listen to others and the degree to which others listen to them. I then invite them to be aware of how they listen to family, friends, and peers during the next week. I also ask them to observe how their cooperating teacher listens to their students in their practicum, how the students listen to their teacher, and how the students listen to each other. They then reflect on their observations and write a response.

Cultivating the capacity to truly listen to students is an essential skill in developing as a teacher. Many students that exhibit less than desirable behaviors in the classroom are actually saying, "I am here. Please notice me. Please acknowledge that I exist." Opening up the space in the classroom for all voices takes time, patience, and skill. It also requires us to slow the learning process down to allow more quiet time for students to contemplate concepts and issues discussed in class. This is particularly important for students who are more introverted by nature, as quite often by the time they have crafted a response to a concept, the extroverts have moved on to the next topic.

Cultivating a mindfulness practice can also contribute to mindful listening and speaking. Hahn and Weare (2017) expresses the importance of this in the classroom:

> The teacher should be able to sit down and listen to the suffering of the students. And the students can come to know the difficulties and the suffering of the teacher and of their fellow students. After they have listened like this, their behaviour will change. The whole class can practice sitting down, breathing, and listening to each other. This is not a waste of time–on the contrary it leads to mutual understanding. Students and teachers will be able to collaborate with each other in making the learning and teaching a joy for both. (p. xxi)

When a class practices mindfulness together, it can lead to profound transformation in the learning community, as the teacher and students become more aware of themselves and each other. This awareness in turn, often leads to positive changes in people's motivations and behaviors.

Sometimes it takes someone else's perspective to make us aware of how much of the talk time we take up. A teacher who uses the inquiry approach in his classroom describes such an event in Mills and Donnelly (2001):

> I had never really contemplated how much I controlled the discourse in the classroom, nor how much my control contributed to an enormous sense of inequity in the class. Furthermore, I had viewed talk as a tool of inquiry. I had never given much thought to inquiring into talk itself or into how we better can utilize talk as learners. During a Friendship Circle in class one day, a student asked if the class could find a way to talk without having to raise their hands. One of the students then replied, "...yeah, Mr. D., you probably control the talk in here a little too much. You say you want us to control ourselves and you don't want to control us. But you decide who can talk when we have discussions. (p. 127)

This student's candid observation of his teacher's behavior prompted the teacher to reflect on his practice, which led to positive changes in his ability to listen to his students. It is important to note that both students felt comfortable enough to speak in this manner to their teacher, which illustrates the importance of creating a safe space in which students can voice concerns in a respectful way. As the entire gamut of personalities and experience exists within the teaching profession, some teachers would not be as comfortable in creating this kind of learning environment.

Facilitating the creation of a learning community is one of the most essential aspects of education, as it lays the foundation for learning to occur. Palmer (1998b) states, "Community, or connectedness, is the principle behind good teaching, but different teachers with different gifts create community in surprisingly diverse ways, using widely divergent methods" (p. 115). This approach reflects holistic pedagogy through the principle of connection.

Finney and Thurgood Sagal (2017) emphasizes the importance of creating a community of learners:

> A community, in its strongest sense, is more than a collection of individuals. It is a living whole, an interconnected group of persons who share a common goal, work together to achieve it, and understand that this takes kindness and mutual support. Creating a caring learning community in the classroom is, perhaps, the most important and valuable work a teacher does. It supports all students to learn more and become stronger and kinder than would be possible in a competitive, hierarchical environment. (p. 159)

As the leaders of communities of learners, we hold the power to either cultivate a positive, healthy learning community or not. When we create a healthy learning community our job becomes easier, as students and teachers work collaboratively rather than engaging in ego battles in which the teacher demands that her/his/their students complete specific tasks and the students either comply or resist. As the students and teacher develop a level of trust between each other, and care and love are given and received, the community bonds deepen.

Although most teachers are overburdened by curriculum, and a plethora of expectations, taking time to purposefully begin the process of community development and maintaining it throughout the year is never a waste of time. As students begin to claim the classroom space as their own (with the teacher) and make decisions as a community regarding their learning processes and ways of interacting with each other, they chart their course. This act can begin the process of not only changing the culture of your classroom, but potentially your school. As you and your students navigate learning experiences together over the course of the year, everyone learns to speak, listen, and collaborate in the spirit of exploration and adventure, and the community begins to feel like a healthy, loving family.

Learning in a Holistic Context: The Findhorn Foundation and Community

Sometimes we connect with a place or a group of people who inspire us on our path as educators. I am fortunate to have been introduced to a community and learning center that reflects my personhood and pedagogy. The Findhorn Foundation and Community (and ecovillage) in northern Scotland is an example of learning in community that is rooted in a specific context with its own unique culture and norms.

The first time that I visited the community I felt as though I had "come home." This was echoed by someone who remarked that the community felt like an outward manifestation of their inner life. I resonate with this sentiment, as there is definitely a special quality to this place. When I enter the community I immediately feel a shift in the atmosphere, as there is a soft, gentle quality paired with a vital pulse. All places have energetic fields that are created by the land and the thoughts and activities of the people living there. Upon arriving in Edinburgh, Scotland, I usually notice a shift as my body begins to relax, even while walking in the streets downtown. In comparison to the city that I work in, (which has a similar population to Edinburgh), this city feels much calmer and more relaxed. People do not tend to rush around in the manner that I am used to experiencing, and I rarely hear a car horn. Once my husband and I take the train up north to the Highlands there is a more profound level of relaxation in my body, and upon entering the Findhorn community, I feel my body becoming more open and softer, as though most of my protective "gear" has been removed. It feels as though the hard edges that I experience in my culture are smoothed away whilst in this community.

Since my early 30s, I have been intrigued with the Findhorn Foundation from both an educational and a spiritual perspective, and after reading the literature on it I felt that it would be an important experience for me both personally and professionally to visit the community. My initial visit was in the Spring of 2012 during a study leave, and during consecutive visits to this community, I have learned much about the development and maintenance of a learning community, the importance of honoring and integrating peoples' inner lives into learning, and how inner listening can affect a person's ability to develop mindful, caring relationships with others and the natural environment. In order to fully appreciate how this community has influenced me, a brief description of this unique center is necessary.

Windswept dunes, craggy rocks, and hippies growing gigantic vegetables are but a few of the images that may come to mind when the name

Findhorn is mentioned. It seems both mythical and firmly rooted at the same time. The Findhorn Foundation is an ecovillage, spiritual community, and international center for holistic education located on the northeast coast of Scotland that has existed for over 50 years. In May of 2012 during a 6-month academic study leave, I enrolled in a 1-week program called Experience Week.

I was particularly interested in the Findhorn Foundation College due to its holistic orientation, but in order to do any further exploration at the Findhorn Foundation College, I was required to enroll in the Experience Week to more fully understand the philosophy behind the community on an experiential level. The Findhorn Foundation brochure boldly stated that the Experience Week can change your world. It sounded like quite a claim.

History and Founding Principles

Eileen and Peter Caddy were the managers of the Cluny Hill Hotel in Forres, Scotland for many years and they developed it into a four-star hotel. In 1962, Peter and Eileen's positions were terminated at the hotel and they decided to move with their three sons and their friend and coworker Dorothy McLean to a caravan park in Findhorn. There they lived in a caravan (what we call a trailer in North America), and as their funds were minimal, Peter began growing a garden in order to feed them. Although they lived on dunes where the land was dry and sandy, they were able to grow unusually large vegetables, following the direct guidance that Eileen received in meditation. At a later date through meditation, Dorothy received information from her communication with the plant spirits or devas. They instructed her on how to plant and tend the gardens with specific details, including what kind of compost to use. Huge plants grew including 40-pound cabbages, and horticulture experts from around the world who were curious about these vegetables began visiting them, making their garden well known throughout the world.

Although they had no intention of starting a community, word of their work spread, and people who were intrigued by what they were doing joined them. As the community developed, they built a community center and a meditation sanctuary based on Eileen's inner guidance. Early on, the Findhorn Foundation welcomed guests who were interested in learning more about living holistically and following inner guidance. The Findhorn Foundation was initiated as a Scottish Charity in 1972 and by the 1980s the community had grown to 300 members.

The Findhorn Ecovillage was initiated during the late 1980s, which included eco-friendly buildings and a wind turbine. It began as an experiment to incorporate what the community had learned about cooperation with nature. Currently there are 90 ecological buildings and in the 1990s, The Living Machine, a biological sewage treatment plant, was installed. The Findhorn Foundation has recorded the lowest eco-footprint of any community in the industrialized world, with their energy footprint being 21% of the national average (they produce 40% more electricity than they require with their wind farm). Their food footprint is 34% of the national average as their diet is mainly local, organic, seasonal vegetables.

Today approximately 500 people live within the community and

> the Findhorn Foundation is the central educational and organizational heart of a widely diversified community of several hundred people, spanning dozens of holistic businesses and initiatives, all linked by a shared positive vision for humanity and the earth, and a commitment to the deep and practical non-doctrinal spirituality established in the Findhorn community by its founders. (http://www.findhorn.org, 2021)

It welcomes over 10,000 visitors annually, with 3,000 residential guests participating in programs, and is the holder of the UN Habitat Best Practice designation.

Although the manner in which the principles of Findhorn are expressed has changed over time, the principles remain central to everything that unfolds in the community. The principles are: to engage in deep inner listening and then to act from that source of wisdom, cocreation with nature's intelligence, and inspired action. Through inner listening, the founders, Dorothy Maclean and Eileen and Peter Caddy, learned to apply the wisdom they received to their gardens and community, which flourished. Through my visits to the community, I was able to more fully understand how people can embody principles like inner listening through engaging in regular meditation, and cocreating with the natural world, as I witnessed it on a daily basis through how gardeners paid great attention to the plants that they were working with in an effort to support their growth. In summary, I learned that being present and aware of who one is, where one is, who one is with, and what is happening, leads to a greater sense of vitality, and as one merges with the environment, a feeling of "being in the flow" arises.

Their understanding of the interdependence of all living things led to the formation of the principles, which continues to help people to contribute positively to the world in a variety of capacities. Dorothy Mclean, who was one of the cofounders of the community, passed away shortly after her

100th birthday in the Winter of 2020. My husband and I were fortunate to meet and spend an afternoon with her several years ago. She had a keen wit, a twinkle in her eye, and she emanated love.

Findhorn Foundation College

According to student Sarah Steinberg, "At Findhorn, the whole community becomes a wonderful classroom" (http://www.findhorn.org, 2021). The main tenets of the Findhorn Foundation College, which was established in 2001 are founded within a paradigm of sustainability and include the combination of experiential learning and mainstream education, the development of basic work and life skills, and inner growth and spiritual development. The main program of study at the Findhorn Foundation College is sustainability, in which all learning occurs within a cooperative learning community including collaboration, cooperative inquiry, and collective learning. The expectation is that students take responsibility for their learning outcomes. The experience of the group is balanced with that of the individual by engaging the inquiry process, and the development of a healthy community is at the forefront of the program.

Developing a Learning Community

The development and maintenance of a healthy learning community is an essential aspect of teaching and learning. The focus on community development occurred immediately upon our arrival in the Findhorn Foundation through hospitality, as someone on the bus who lived in the park, took us straight to the reception area where we were warmly greeted by one of our focalisers (their term for a group leader). He gave us time to relax, fill in a few forms, and then took us to the guest lodge that we would share with five other people. The guest lodge had a large kitchen and lounge area in between the bedrooms and washrooms, at which point I noted, "Oh, community within community." Sharing accommodation with others was one way of creating community among group members, as we ate breakfast together and shared the space for the week. Many insightful, stimulating conversations occurred during our time together in the lodge.

Hospitality and Synchronicity

This occurs in many ways, and several years ago during a visit, my husband and I experienced it on our first day. There are many synchronistic events that happen whenever I stay in this community. On the day of our arrival we were just stepping outside of our door and I heard someone say, "Tucker! Lisa!" and there was our friend Marlene holding a large vase brimming with beautiful flowers. She was standing beside her car, as she was picking up some friends and taking them to the airport. She had given the flowers to them, and as they were leaving, she was about to deliver them to our place for us to enjoy them next. What a beautiful way to start our day!

Mid-morning my husband wanted to find a good book to read, so we went to their store, The Phoenix, in search of a book. He was unsuccessful in his quest, so we continued to the coffee shop to have a prearranged meeting with a community member who had written a book on sustainable communities. We had an interesting conversation with him, and he told us that he had written a book on his experience in the community and that he would drop off a copy for us. Sure enough, shortly after returning to our accommodation he arrived with a copy of his book. These synchronistic events are expressed well by the band, The Police:

> Synchronicity
> A connecting principle
> Linked to the invisible
> Almost imperceptible
> Something inexpressible
> Science insusceptible
> Logic so inflexible
> Causally connectable
> Nothing is invincible
> We know, they know me
> Extrasensory
> Synchronicity
> A star fall, a phone call
> It joins all
> (Gordon Sumner, 1983)

The initial tour of the community contributed to my feeling of "coming home," as the community literally is a park. There are lots of old growth trees, shrubs, flowers, and no fences between homes. The community is designed in such a manner that people do not park their cars beside their homes, but in specified parking lots. This is purposeful in that the roads are dedicated to pedestrians and those on bicycles. This purposeful design creates opportunities for community members to stop and interact with each other, which contributes to a thriving community. There are many sustainable homes, including a straw bale house, others with living roofs, and houses made out of old whisky barrels or vats. Evidence of sustainability is at every turn including three wind turbines that supply electricity for the community. The inclusion of weaving, pottery, and art studios demonstrates their commitment to the arts, and the Moray Art Center is also situated on the site. The focus on beauty is evident throughout the community in the artistically constructed stone and sod roof nature sanctuary and in the community center with pastel designs painted on a variety of walls, and concrete pathways around the center with inlaid stone mosaics. The Universal Hall, which hosts conferences and concerts, is a spectacular building with a hand-carved stone exterior, a geodesic roof, and stained glass windows in the entry.

There is a thoughtful approach to creating community for workshop participants, including engaging in trust games, working together, and having fun as a group. Nature outings, group work, sacred dance, and meditation are also part of the week with a focus on living in community and engaging it as fully as possible. Based on this experience, I have incorporated several games into my teaching at the beginning of the year to help my students to get to know each other and to begin the process of learning how to work together. Community was also developed among the workshop participants during sharing at mealtimes in which rich conversation helped people to create deeper connections with each other.

What impressed me the most was how heart centered most of the people were, and during our initial sessions with our group several people wept as they shared their stories. The understanding in the group was that when people shared about themselves, the other group members listened without interrupting with questions or advice giving. This provided a safe space in which people could express themselves freely. It is a place where people are allowed to be who they are, and an atmosphere of trust and genuine care is extended to community members and visitors. I feel that the power of this is that it releases people from having to be defensive and it leads to openness, which contributes to heart-centered communication.

The Balance of Inner and Outer Lives

It is an expectation that the community members all engage in some form of inner listening on a regular basis, whether that is meditation, walking in the woods, doing tai chi, yoga, or other practices. This act of going inward and becoming familiar with and learning about one's inner life informs how people interact with others. Participants in the foundation's workshops are invited to meditation sessions held at several times during the day, and then spend time in service departments 3 or 4 days a week, including the kitchen, home care, or maintenance. This work time was appropriately called Love in Action and was one of the most powerful aspects of my experience there. Once our group had gathered, I noticed a beautiful arrangement of flowers and foliage in a shallow bowl with a lit candle in the middle, on the table. We sat in a circle, became quiet, and became aware of the energy of the group. This was followed by a brief sharing to establish where everyone was at in the morning. The specific jobs were then decided upon based on peoples' needs and energy levels on that particular day. I found this to be such a simple, yet effective way of determining what work people would engage in during the day. It followed people's natural rhythms and shifts on a daily basis, and genuinely honored the individuals within the larger group.

Learning/Sharing in Circles

The inclusion of the inner lives of participants was also evident in the learning activities within the community. Most of the facilitators of workshops began each session by having a sharing circle, in which people had an opportunity to share anything that they deemed important, including letting others know how they were doing. This also gave the facilitator important information regarding how to focus the teaching for the day, and it was this responsiveness to the learners that made a positive difference in our learning experience. I have rarely witnessed such heartfelt, genuine sharing by people who were strangers.

Rituals

I had a very powerful experience during a workshop called Spiritual Practice With Clay. Our leader Craig was a potter and it was evident that he was passionate about working with clay. On the first day of the weeklong workshop we walked out to the Findhorn Bay and he dug up clay which we put into plastic bags to carry back with us. We used this clay throughout the week and were given complete freedom to create whatever arose for us. This led to some powerful moments including that of a woman who was finalizing a divorce from her husband. She created a series of clay forms, allowed them to dry, and then on another day took them to the bay, and created a ceremony in which she placed them on the shore, and watched them gradually dissolve and become part of the seabed. This example demonstrates the power of inviting and supporting learners to engage with concepts or disciplines on a personal level.

Midweek we took our clay and tools into what Craig called an earth lodge that he had built many years ago. The earth lodge is a semi-subterranean structure with wooden poles forming the roof, covered with a tarp. There was a firepit in the center and a hole in the roof through which the smoke exited. Craig lit the fire and for what seemed like hours, we sat around it and worked with the clay on a large slab of wood resting on our laps. I recall everyone being very quiet, and about an hour after working with the clay he asked us if we wanted to go to his house for some ginger tea. No one replied, and we continued working as he went home to brew the tea and returned with it. Not only did he bring tea, but he also brought his didgeridoo which is often used for shamanic work. Being from Australia, he was quite an accomplished player. There we were partially in the earth, sitting around a fire working with clay, listening to the sounds of animals and nature emitting from the didgeridoo. As I worked with the clay and put my creation on a screen near the fire to heat it, I imagined my ancestors doing the same thing with clay and felt as though I was deeply connected to them in a way previously unimagined. It was one of the most powerful experiences of my life and was a prelude to my initiation into shamanic practice some years later.

The Gift of Inner Listening

The effects of engaging in a regular practice of inner listening are evident in this community through how people interact with others. There is a heightened degree of awareness, or as people in the western world call it "mindfulness," which leads to greater levels of responsiveness to people, situations, and environments. When people are in the present moment, there is less of a need to defend one's stance on an issue, or to control a situation, and a greater receptivity to others' ideas and opinions. Until very recently when the community grew in numbers, most of the decisions were made using the consensus process, rather than voting on issues and allowing decisions to be made based on the majority. During meetings if a challenging issue arose, participants would take a period of time to meditate and access their inner source of wisdom, and then bring that wisdom and guidance to the group as the meeting continued. Rather than making decisions based on whose voice is the loudest, the inner listening that people in this community engage in contributes to decision-making that goes beyond the level of personal and collective egos.

A synergy exists in the community that is palpable, and according to Hawken (1975), "Synergy here means a social state in which the whole is greater than the sum of its parts. In other words, it is describing a state in which the individual in a group is greater than himself alone, with broader awareness and creative potential" (p. 308).

I noticed that people in the Findhorn community are very observant, genuine, and they go the extra mile to help others, as was exemplified with my husband one day. He was working in the kitchen and a few of the people noticed that his shoulder was giving him problems. A lot of the people that live there are also professionals in the areas of bodywork, naturopathy, and homeopathy. With his permission, one of the people worked on his shoulder for awhile. Then during lunch someone came over and found the name of an osteopath in a neighboring town. One of the people in our guest lodge called the osteopath and volunteered to drive my husband after dinner. I was very moved by the level of genuine caring by the people in the community.

During periods of working, I also observed that it took people some time to get into their jobs, as they spent around 20 minutes gathering as a group, attuning, and determining who would be responsible for which job on a given day. As people weeded gardens or repainted trim on windows, or vacuumed the floor in a dining room, no one seemed to be in a hurry. It felt as though great care and attention was given to whatever the task was. This is quite counter to the dominant work ethic in North America, in which people are rewarded for working at a faster pace and for longer hours.

This heightened level of awareness is also evident in how community members work with the natural environment. Their understanding of and respect for the land and all plants and animals living on it contributes to the health of the entire community. They are co-creators with the natural world. One day I was with a team of gardeners and our job was to transplant some small shrubs. Under the guidance of the head gardener, we stood beside each plant, sensed how it wanted to be placed in its new home, and gently communicated to it that its new home would provide it with more space for its roots to spread out so that it would receive more nutrients.

The focus on interspecies communication came to the fore during my first visit. One of the gardeners talked to us about their system of growing vegetables and someone asked how they handled pests in the garden. She relayed the story of a particular mole that had been eating the carrots and parsnips. She had a communication via thoughts with the mole and asked it to move to a nice pile of soil away from the greenhouse, as it was full of lovely, tasty worms. After a few days she checked the greenhouse and there was no evidence of the mole.

This intrigued me, as a week before we left on our trip to Scotland my husband found several mounds created by a mole around the foundation of our home. My father offered to set a trap for the mole while we were away, which I did not feel very good about, but he did so. Soon after the gardener's talk I communicated with the mole on our property and asked it to move to a hill of soil about 100 feet from our house where it would find tasty grubs. When we returned from our journey, I was hesitant to check the trap, but when I did there was no mole in it. A few weeks later my husband and I observed that there were no more mounds around our house, as the mole had indeed moved away. This was an interesting exploration for me as I realized that there are many ways in which to live and work with animals in a positive manner that I had not previously considered.

The community members' practices of inner listening, which leads to greater levels of awareness, helps to create a gentle, caring, and supportive environment in which people work, learn, play, and celebrate together. I also invite students to adopt a contemplative practice throughout the year in the classes that I teach. The rationale for this is that it is an opportunity for students to develop a set of mental skills and socio-emotional dispositions that will not only benefit them personally, but will enhance their presence as teachers and may become a form of self-care that they can cultivate prior to entering the teaching profession. Schoeberlein and Sheth (2009) speaks to mindfulness, "Master teachers are mindful teachers, aware of themselves and attuned to their students. *Mindful teaching* nurtures a learning community in which students flourish academically, emotionally, and socially—and teachers thrive professionally and personally" (p. 1).

Through my own practice of inner listening, I try to be as fully present as possible to my students during our classes to create a safe, open space in which all may feel comfortable to explore and express ideas freely. J. Miller (2000) supports contemplative practice as a way for teachers to deepen their presence, as "teachers who cannot bring their authentic presence to the classroom each day, who cannot attune themselves empathetically to their students are ill-equipped to give of themselves or respond appropriately to students' needs" (p. 121). I have observed that as my students and I commit to being more fully present not only to ourselves and each other, but to our subject matter, that learning deepens.

This unique and sustainable learning center provides people with opportunities to live and learn within a dynamic community, and they continue to experiment with ways of living that allows all beings to flourish. I have deepened my knowledge regarding how to develop and maintain a learning community, the importance of honoring and integrating peoples' inner lives into learning, and how inner listening can positively affect a person's ability to develop mindful, nurturing relationships with others and the natural environment.

Teaching is a complex profession and in order for true exploration and deep learning to occur, a healthy, caring, and sustainable learning community must be developed. My experience has revealed that the guiding principles of the Findhorn Foundation have the potential to contribute to the creation of such communities. As the teacher is responsible for setting the tone for the learning community, Palmer (1998b) reminds us that "the courage to teach is the courage to keep one's heart open in those very moments when the heart is asked to hold more than it is able so that teacher and students and subject can be woven into the fabric of community that learning, and living, require" (p. 11).

Developing a healthy, dynamic community within my classroom has been greatly informed by my experiences in the Findhorn Foundation and community. When I left the Findhorn Foundation my heart was open, and as the brochure claimed, the experience that I had there did change my world.

4

Being Real

Paying Attention

"Real isn't how you are made," said the Skin Horse. "It's a thing that happens to you.

When a child loves you for a long, long time, not just to play with, but REALLY loves you, then you become Real."

"Does it hurt?" asked the Rabbit.

"Sometimes," said the Skin Horse, for he was always truthful. "When you are Real you don't mind being hurt."

        —Margery Williams (1944), *The Velveteen Rabbit*

The classroom can be a very busy and noisy place. Five days a week, for 5 hours or more, 20–40 people meet in a relatively small space with the intention of learning. Each person has a unique personality, abilities, energy level, and motivation. The person charged with teaching them, is in essence like the conductor of a symphony, keeping everyone together and

Flourishing in the Holistic Classroom, pages 59–81
Copyright © 2021 by Information Age Publishing

59

harmonious, with the goal of learning. This is no small feat. Until relatively recently in the history of public schooling, students were "kept in line" initially through physical punishment, then when that was abolished, through deterrents in the form of grades, activities being taken away, having to stay in during recess, and being assigned extra homework.

Chapter 4 explores the role of mindfulness practice in the classroom, which when engaged on a regular basis helps a person to connect with their true self or soul. This movement on the spiral is leading to the center—the person's inner world. This chapter also addresses how the presence of the teacher influences the learning community, followed by a discussion on how educators experience fear and vulnerability. Mindfulness practice and teacher presence have the potential to cultivate the core features of flourishing, which are interest and engagement, as well as the additional feature of resilience.

With the advent of technologies of varying types, many students have become distracted from their learning in school. This is partially due to experiencing an overload of information from all angles; they are plugged in 24/7. There is currently a movement in public education to help students to become more aware of themselves, others, their surroundings, and their learning. This is often referred to as mindfulness. This chapter explores many facets of mindfulness beginning with the description of how I introduced mindfulness practice to my students in the early years, and more recently, in a preservice teacher education program. Teacher presence is then explored in relation to mindfulness practice. This is followed by an exploration of feeling, facing, and dissipating fear, and the role that vulnerability plays in cultivating positive relationships that foster a learning community in which all participants flourish.

Pausing . . . Being . . . Contemplative Practice in the Classroom

Preservice teacher programs place great emphasis on theory and technique, both of which play crucial roles in teacher identity formation. This emphasis on externally acquired knowledge can mean that the inner life of the person who is developing into a teacher tends to be either minimally addressed or ignored altogether. Since entering the teaching profession in 1987, I have been keenly aware of my inner development, and the importance of teaching to the inner life of the students in my classroom. This is a short chronicle of how contemplative practice has influenced and become an integral part of my work.

When I ask my students in a preservice teacher education program that I teach to describe a teacher that was influential to them, they typically share that their teacher was caring, patient, enthusiastic, interested in who they were, went out of their way to help them when they needed it, mentored them, and challenged them accordingly. Palmer (1998b) addresses this by stating that "good teaching cannot be reduced to technique; good teaching comes from the identity and integrity of the teacher" (p. 10). We know that master teachers have this capacity for connectedness and teach from their wholeness, or true self, thus it seems logical that we support pre-teachers in developing these qualities. If we want teachers to be effective in their classrooms, and for them and their students to be healthy, happy, and engaged in the learning process, the inner life of preservice and in-service teachers must be given as much, if not more, emphasis than theory and technique in both preservice teacher programs and in professional development for teachers.

As a teacher in the early years, I taught from a holistic perspective, although I was not introduced to the literature on holistic education until some 15 years later. I designed my curriculum thematically and taught through projects, ensuring that the children were exploring ideas and concepts with their mind, body, and spirit. I experienced deep joy as I supported the natural curiosity of my students.

I incorporated a self-esteem program into my curriculum in order to help the students to learn more about themselves and each other, and to contribute to developing a caring, supportive learning community. Many of my students had challenging home lives, and I intuited that they would benefit from a regular meditative practice, and in particular, that having quiet time during the day would help them to connect to their true self. During my third year of teaching, I naively approached my principal requesting to hold regular meditation sessions with my students, and he responded with a decisive, "No." I understood his reticence at allowing a fairly inexperienced teacher to initiate such a practice, as meditation was perceived as being suspiciously "New Age" in the 1980s. Because I had been exploring meditation and other contemplative practices and understood the potential these had for self-discovery and inner knowing, cultivating calmness and compassion, and overall well-being, I initiated the practice despite my principal's response, and called it "quiet time."

Quiet time occurred in the morning following the school wide announcements, and again right after lunch time, or prior to dismissal at the end of the day. The practice consisted of me and my students sitting quietly at our desks or together on the carpet in our meeting area, with our eyes either open or closed, and attending to the inflow and outflow of our breath. Each session was approximately ten minutes in duration. Over time I observed that the children's energy levels softened, they began to treat each other with increasing levels of kindness, and they developed a greater ability to focus and concentrate on their learning. They responded very positively to the quiet time and began to request it when they sensed that they needed it.

> *"What day is it?" asked Winnie the Pooh.*
> *"It's today," squeaked Piglet.*
> *"My favorite day," said Pooh.*
> —*The Adventures of Winnie the Pooh* by A. A. Milne (1926)

This was a transformative experience for me as a novice teacher, and some 30 years later I am experiencing a similar transformation in my classrooms as I teach students in the middle year of a teacher education program. Nearly a decade ago, I returned to a regular meditation practice as an act of survival. What had been a very positive work environment suddenly became a challenging place for me, as the new direction offered by the interim administration was counter to my work as a holistic educator. However, this sociopolitical context was in sharp contrast to what occurred in my classroom. My classroom was a haven for me, as I enjoyed working with my students, and I credit them with being partially responsible for my decision to remain in my position. I was suffering and felt desperate to escape my situation. As I already had experience with meditation, I decided that I would return to my practice in the hope that I would become rooted and strong, and that this would help me to navigate the difficult circumstance that I found myself in.

My daily practice consisted of meditating for either 40 minutes prior to going to work or a 20-minute session prior to teaching, and another 20-minute session in the evening. This period of contemplative practice helped me to gradually become more rooted, calm, and prepared for the day. The other practice that I engaged in was saying the following mantra every morning before entering my classroom, "Today I will be as present as possible to my students." Reciting this mantra assisted me in remaining in the present moment as much as possible during my workday and helped to keep me focused on the positive aspects of my job. My focus for the next year and a half was first, on my well-being, and second, on my efficacy as a teacher. The contemplative practice became a form of self-care and assisted me in becoming more heart-centered and staying in that center, despite my instinct to protect myself in increasingly difficult circumstances. I felt as though I had become a spiritual warrior out of necessity.

Meditation is one aspect of contemplative practice. Contemplative practice is about having a direct experience with yourself and your life. It is about paying attention to and being aware of what is happening inside of yourself and around you. It is characterized by increased awareness and openness to experiences. Contemplation can happen in many forms, from reading poetry and allowing the words to wash over you rather than trying to analyze the poem, to walking in a forest or sitting on a park bench and letting nature awaken you. Contemplation is about pausing . . . being . . . awareness.

While my first reason for returning to a regular meditation practice was self-preservation, I became aware that my inner work was having a positive effect on my efficacy in the classroom. My intention of being as fully present as possible to my students was beginning to bear fruit and I began to observe that students were responding positively to my calmness and increased presence. J. Miller (2014) addresses the effect of meditation on teacher presence,

> From the perspective of teacher education, meditation is important to how we approach teaching. If teaching is ego-based it can become a frustrating series of mini-battles with students. The classroom becomes focused around the issue of control. If we teach from our original self (eg., our Buddha nature), teaching becomes a fulfilling and enriching experience. (p. 43)

I began to teach more and more from my original self, was more heart-centered, relaxed, and present to my students, and everything in my classroom seemed to flow more smoothly.

During this period of time, I also had contact through email and in person at conferences with mentors in the field of holistic education such as J. Miller. J. Miller (2014) had been teaching his students contemplative practice successfully for decades and states,

> I have witnessed many small miracles that have occurred as a result of contemplative practices. Some of my students find they have more restful sleep, others report it makes them less reactive when a student acts out in the classroom, but most simply find that contemplative practice brings more serenity into their lives. (p. 3)

One of J. Miller's (2014) students shares how the mindfulness practice that is part of his course affected her:

> It changed my life a lot in many ways from the inside. I know I'm less anxious and worried, and whenever I let my mind dwell on the future or the past, I get upset again, and then I have to bring myself back. When I'm thinking of the past or the future, and they are equally painful . . . I can simply bring my-

self to the present with a few breaths, breathing deeply, and then focusing on the moment and just doing it without letting thought distract me; that's very helpful for me. (p. 135)

Conversations with colleagues who taught holistically provided me with greater conviction that introducing contemplative practice to my students would not only be possible, but potentially beneficial for them.

I began to ponder how I would integrate contemplative practice into the course that I taught. The course curriculum included teaching students to create lesson and unit plans, classroom management, a variety of teaching strategies, assessment practices, and other practical aspects of the teaching profession. The work in this course supports students in their practice experience in schools one full day per week. In the process of deciding how I would introduce contemplative practice to my students, I faced a few obstacles; namely fear and doubt. This included wondering what my colleagues would think of me, and how my students would respond. I ruminated over being judged by colleagues as not being academically rigorous and wondered if my students might think that I was wasting their time with contemplative practice, as it isn't typically part of curricula in teacher education programs.

While I was feeling fearful, I also recognized the importance of introducing the practice to preservice teachers, and in 2013 I took the plunge. I spent an entire class talking to my students about contemplation, including sharing research on mindfulness practice, and then proceeded to walk them through a variety of contemplative practices, including noticing and following the breath, using mantras, visualization, and walking meditation. I drew most of these exercises from my experience with meditation and mindfulness practice over the course of 2 decades. Following each practice, I invited the students to share their experiences. I was admittedly nervous during that first class as I was aware of being as fully present as possible as we experienced a variety of contemplative practices and noticing the fears and doubts that I experienced throughout the class as I tuned into my students' responses to each exercise. Thankfully, at the end of each class, several students approached me and either thanked me for introducing them to the practices or let me know that they already engaged in a contemplative practice.

From that class on, we sat for 3 minutes at the beginning of a 50-minute class in silence. I invited my students to choose the practice that most resonated with them and to do so either with their eyes open or closed. During the first few classes, I had some trepidation, wondering whether they would be receptive, or thought I was wasting their time, and as I had these thoughts I returned to my breath. Some students fidgeted for the first few sessions and I could sense their discomfort, but they gradually slipped into the routine. We had several insightful conversations about the difficulty that some of them had with being still and not talking or using electronic devices, and I began to sense that for many of my students this may have been a rare moment of pausing and unplugging. As our practice became established, what I observed was that they had increased levels of focus and concentration in class, as well as being more present to each other. This contributed to an increasingly respectful, caring, learning community.

As I deepened my regular contemplative practice, I felt more present to my students and more aware of the learning experiences that we were engaged in. This led to a more relaxed and joyful experience for me, as I realized that I was developing the ability to be more open to the unfolding experience in the classroom. Because my students also felt this, the usual posture of attacking and defending ideas often present within academia shifted. Students still challenged ideas and assumptions, which is an expectation, but they did it with an attitude of genuinely wanting to gain further understanding, rather than simply putting others' ideas down in an attempt to prop up their own egos. They were interacting with each other and the subject matter, not solely from an egotistic stance, but from their hearts as well.

I became aware of my students' attention and focus increasing during class discussions and regular group discussions on specific topics, and as Barbezat and Bush (2014) note, "A key element in solving any problem is attention. Anyone who has attempted to solve complex problems knows the intense concentration and attention required. Contemplative exercises hone this skill" (p. 12).

I also observed another unexpected benefit for me. That year I taught three consecutive 50-minute classes beginning at 8:30 in the morning, which was very intense and required a great degree of concentration and focus. I found that the contemplative practice provided me with an opportunity to pause...release the energy and experiences of the previous class...and prepare for the new group of students. I felt refreshed and ready for each class.

Throughout the course in casual conversations, I was heartened by the predominance of positive responses to the contemplative practice, and this gave me support to continue and deepen the practice the following year. I spent the summer reflecting on these student responses and refining my teaching practice.

The next year, I began in a manner similar to the previous year, explaining contemplative practice, including the many benefits for teachers and students. Schoeberlein and Sheth (2009) detail the benefits for teachers of mindfulness practice as: "improves focus and awareness, increases responsiveness to students' needs, promotes emotional balance, supports stress management and stress reduction, supports healthy relationships at work and home, enhances classroom climate and supports overall well-being" (p. 9). They continue describing the benefits for students including:

> supports "readiness to learn," promotes academic performance, strengthens attention and concentration, reduces anxiety before testing, promotes self-reflection and self-calming, improves classroom participation by supporting impulse control, provides tools to reduce stress, enhances social and emotional learning, fosters pro-social behaviours and healthy relationships, and supports holistic well-being. (p. 9)

Contemplative practice including mindfulness has these and more benefits for students, and in the academic context I felt that it was appropriate to share these research findings with my students, as all teaching approaches must be justified regarding how they will benefit student learning. However, this practice has a much deeper purpose than is usually discussed in the context of education. Hanh, a Vietnamese monk, describes the meaning for him and the people in his community,

> In Plum Village the practice of mindfulness is taught not as a tool, but as a path. Mindfulness is a way of living that we are always cultivating and deepening. Mindfulness is not a means to arrive at an end; It is not a tool for us to use to get better outcomes later—whether those outcomes are greater happiness or improved grades. (Hahn & Weare, 2017, p. xxvii)

My students' entry into the contemplative practice was consistent with that of the previous year, and by the third week of classes the practice had been established. At times they requested a longer session, often due to pressure building prior to exams, so we spent more time on those particular occasions. This indicated to me that they were beginning to recognize the benefit of the practice, and that they were developing an awareness of when they would benefit from engaging in mindfulness.

The classroom community also began to have a more joyful feel to it, which of course is very conducive to the well-being and learning of students and teachers. Hahn describes:

> If you're joyful, happy, and aware, you light up the lamp of happiness and joy in others, because in each of us there is a seed of mindfulness, a seed of awareness. This is an art, and it's not difficult. As a teacher, you can perform

that miracle in just a few seconds, and you can make the students in your class happy. (Hahn & Weare, 2017, p. xx)

Students that are happy have a much greater chance of learning than those who are miserable and under stress. Unlike Western education systems, which primarily focus on creating adults who will be compliant workers and eager consumers in an effort to increase their GDP (gross domestic product), some countries have a clear focus on not only their country's GDP but the well-being of their citizens. The country of Bhutan has focused on the happiness and well-being of their citizens and call it GNH (gross national happiness). This focus has become integrated into their education system, and J. Miller (2014) was invited along with 23 educators to work with the officials and teachers in Bhutan to help implement their goals. J. Miller (2014) describes the four pillars of GNH:

GNH includes four pillars and nine domains within each pillar: 1. Sustainable and equitable socio-economic development (living standards, health, and education), 2. Environmental conservation, 3. Promotion of culture (psychological well-being, time use, cultural resilience, and diversity, and community vitality), and 4. Enhancement of good governance (which includes caring for the people, accountability, transparency, and other attributes). (p. 16)

During the first few classes, I encountered some of the same fears that I had in the previous year but experienced greater success in remaining present. A colleague who was presenting to my students during one of our classes remarked to them how courageous I was in establishing a contemplative practice with them in an academic setting.

In casual conversation with my students they have expressed that their contemplative practice helps them to focus in class, that it makes them calm, that it helps them with anxiety during test writing, and others have reported that it sets the tone for their entire day. Anxiety and depression have become heightened on most university campuses in the last decade and contemplative practice has been proven to decrease levels of both as cited in numerous studies. Barbezat and Bush (2014) note,

In a series of carefully constructed experiments, Shauna Shapiro and colleagues have shown that students exposed to eight to ten weeks of meditation practices significantly decreased their levels of anxiety and depression (even during especially stressful finals periods) compared to carefully selected control groups. (p. 27)

Another benefit of contemplative practice is that it contributes to inner knowledge. It is a way for us to more fully understand our values, needs, desires, and our true purpose in life. Self-knowledge is crucial for teachers as they navigate the course for their students on a daily basis. The more keenly they know and understand themselves, the more able they are to know and understand their students. J. Miller (2018) describes:

> One important reason for including contemplative practices such as mindfulness in teacher education is that it can be a form of self-learning. For example, mindfulness meditation is based on the notion that we can learn and grow by simply watching our own experience. As we notice our own thoughts and agendas, we can gain deeper insight into ourselves and the nature of experience. In this context, mindfulness is a form of inquiry. In contrast, the model for much learning at the university level is that the professor and the text are the authority and the student must learn from these authorities. Mindfulness meditation provides one alternative to this model and instead recognizes that we can learn from ourselves and our own experience. (p. 95)

One of the key findings of the study in spirituality in higher education at the UCLA Higher Education Research Institute was that students were asking for support in their search for meaning and purpose in their lives. In addition, more than two-thirds of the student body considered it either very important, or essential, that their college contribute to their self-understanding (Astin et al., 2010). Through a regular contemplative practice, students have an opportunity to begin to listen to their inner voice and begin honing their purpose in life.

During the last decade I have come to recognize the potential for contemplative practice to transform learning environments. The adoption of a meditation practice on my part has supported me in teaching from my original or true self, and I feel more relaxed and connected to my students and our subject matter. I have also observed that through the regular contemplative practice as a learning community, that we have deepened our connections with ourselves, each other, and our subject material, and there is a deeper level of trust, caring, and joy in our interactions with each other.

The experience of integrating contemplative practice into my teaching has been one of the most transformative experiences of my teaching career, and hopefully has been transformative for my students as well. As always, my students are my teachers, and I have learned that regular contemplative practice can transform learning environments by providing students and teachers with a way of encountering their true self, by giving themselves hospitality and self-care, and in the process developing greater capacity for relating to themselves and others by being more fully present. This manifests in thoughtful, caring, insightful, and trusting communities of learners. To come to truly know, not only ourselves, but others, and the subject matter that we are studying, can best be accomplished from our wholeness. Contemplative practice is a doorway into understanding the fullness and depth of not only ourselves, but of life and learning.

Teacher Presence

Teaching is a highly complex art form. It requires knowledge of theory, techniques, and strategies, which then intersect with the human that is actually teaching. It is the difference between the teacher in the Peanuts cartoons, who drones on, "wa, wa, wa, wa" and the scene from the movie *The Dead Poet's Society* in which Robin Williams gathers his students closely together and asks them what their verse will be. Teaching requires both mastery of subject, theory, technique, and the ability to be genuine, present, and vulnerable with students, rather than "playing" the role of teacher.

In faculties of education preservice teachers have ample training in theory, technique, and strategies. Based on my experience and research, the key qualities that teachers can cultivate to increase their efficacy in the classroom are not often focused upon, yet it is these very qualities that make the difference between someone who becomes a good teacher and someone who becomes a master teacher that students will remember for years to come. Some of these qualities include being caring, accommodating, fair, good listeners, clear communicators, enthusiastic, humorous, patient, flexible, encouraging, supportive, genuine, and vulnerable. These qualities or attributes all contribute to the teacher's presence. J. Miller (2018) shares:

> Presence is an elusive quality but we know it when we encounter it in another person who listens with their whole being. Genuine presence has a healing quality. Presence is critically important in teaching; the teacher who is able to be present to students creates an environment where real learning can occur. When we reflect on teachers who made a difference in our lives, it is often their presence rather than their pedagogy that made that difference. (p. 86)

Teaching is above all else a human endeavor. It hinges on positive relationships that are based on care, trust, acceptance, support, and love. One of the most powerful ways of cultivating presence and warm heartedness in the classroom is through developing a regular mindfulness practice. Alderfer (2015) supports this as: "Therein lies an openness of receiving and growing in love, a spaciousness of heart and mind that is always unstuck, always whole. The practice of mindfulness cultivates this unfolding process" (p. xviii). The presence of the teacher has a powerful effect on the students and their ability to learn, and as Alderfer (2015) describes, "At the heart of mindfulness rests the ever-present wholeness of being-accessible once the thinking mind has calmed down, when logic and intellect have found a respite" (p. xxx). This is a significant insight and brings to mind the experience of sitting on a park bench with a friend watching the ducks in the pond. It is a peaceful feeling to sit with your friend, saying very little to each other, and just being. Mindfulness, therefore, is about "being." In essence, we can only be as caring, supportive, genuine, and open-minded with others as we are with ourselves. Mindfulness can be viewed as an act of hospitality to ourselves and to others.

For me, one of the keys of teaching is based on my interactions with students from my true self to their true self. It is about being genuine and heart-full in the classroom. It is about discovering each student's abilities and interests and encouraging them to develop them. Much of this stems from being mindful, present, or aware of the self, the students, and the attending subject matter that we are engaging. This of course, is counter to the dominant narrative in education in North America, which is based on being head-centered. Alderfer (2015) shares:

> Heartfulness is an emerging term and may more accurately describe the concept of mindfulness within a framework of Western thought. This might be, in part, because in the West wisdom is thought of as being in the mind, which is considered to be in the head. On the Asian subcontinent, where I have lived and taught most of the past twenty years, the seat of wisdom is considered to be in the heart rather than the head. (p. xvi)

I have become increasingly aware that when I teach in a head-centered mode I can facilitate learning, be knowledgeable, inspiring, and clever. However, when I teach in a mindful and heart-centered manner, because I am more connected to my inner self rather than exclusively to the content, I become less of a talking head and more of an authentic human. This is a profound experience for me, and as I observe my students I can tell that I am connecting with them in a deeper way. The best way that I can describe the feeling of this experience is that I am fully present not only to myself, but to my students, and the content. I am centered in a moment in time and space that is simultaneously timeless. This enables me to more fully respond to whatever the moment holds. Byrnes (2012) shares,

Teaching with mindful awareness is a quality of mind that allows a teacher to attend simultaneously to both the minute details and wholeness in a moment. Mindfulness focuses on the minute, the immediate, while awareness offers a more global picture. (p. 24)

Hahn and Weare (2017) express that "mindfulness can help us learn the embodied skills that can support us to stay solid, relaxed, open-minded, calm, and reflective so that we do not take challenges personally and can better manage our own emotional stress" (p. 217).

Mindfulness practice then, supports teachers in being less reactive and more responsive with students. This is of utmost importance, as when a teacher reacts to student behaviors rather than pausing and then responding, it can lead to words and actions that not only amplify the charged situation, but potentially creates cause for disciplinary action towards the teacher. I often relay to my students that where we have psychological wounds, our students will find those places and push all of our buttons, hence regular inner reflection and development has a direct correlation to our efficacy in the classroom. The ability to stay present to our students is described by Finney and Thurgood Sagal (2017):

When we are comfortable with ourselves in the world, we do not have a need to manipulate others with false praise or to pretend to be someone we are not. Authenticity means that we have a sense of who we are and have no need to repress any part of ourselves. By being ourselves, we are able to dedicate our energy to being present rather than using some of our energy to play a role or hide who we truly are. (p. 22)

J. Miller (2014) relays a poignant story of teacher presence:

The Zen Roshi, Shunryu Suzuki, tells a wonderful story about the presence of a teacher (Chadwick, 1999). He was head of a temple in Japan and was looking for a kindergarten teacher for the temple school. He repeatedly tried to convince a woman to take the job but she refused. Finally he said to her, "You don't have to do anything, just stand there." When he said that, she accepted the position. He was convinced that her presence alone would make a difference in the lives of the children. Of course, she did not just stand in the classroom, but Suzuki-roshi identified this important element in teaching. (p. 13)

Teacher presence then, is a key aspect of education, as we work towards becoming as present as possible to our students and their learning. Nava (2001) describes that the nature of the educator's consciousness is the most important factor in his or her development. We can call this consciousness "full presence." Full presence is the mind's natural state, the presence of all that we are, the full presence of body, mind, and consciousness—a state of total awareness. (p. 154)

This state of total awareness creates an atmosphere of calmness, receptivity, caring, and open-mindedness, as one's ego is not at the fore, but rather observes the full presence of being. O'Donohue (1999) speaks to the power of presence, "It is the art of belonging to one's soul that keeps one's presence aflame. From this belonging comes the light of inspiration and vision, which cannot be manufactured, only received" (p. 66). He elaborates on this aspect, "There is no forcing of presence; they do not drive themselves outwards to impress or ingratiate themselves" (p. 68).

If full awareness or presence is such a key aspect of teaching, it seems logical that its cultivation be included in preservice teacher programs. Through bringing our full presence to our students and our discipline, we create a space or a container in which deep learning can flourish. Cohen (2015) sums this up beautifully, "I believe that presence is equivalent to love. Giving full presence to another is, I believe, the greatest gift a person can offer. Another way of saying this is to equate presence with full attention" (p. 37). Through cultivating mindfulness, heartfulness, and presence, we are better equipped to give students our full attention to a greater extent. This may mean of course that we slow our teaching down, or that we may not cover as much of the curriculum as is mandated. It is a choice that teachers make on a daily basis, and to me is the difference between choosing to eat a smorgasbord or having a feast. I choose the feast at every opportunity.

Working With Fear: Being Vulnerable

During the time in which I began introducing mindfulness to my students, I also wanted to initiate a regular "drop in" mindfulness group for students in the faculty of education (ultimately, I did not receive the support to bring this to fruition). After discussing it with the dean, he recommended that I discuss my proposal with a colleague who had been a meditator for many years. I met with my colleague and described the mindfulness practice that I was doing with my students, and he seemed quite shocked that I could sit at the front of the room with my eyes closed in front of all of my students. His comment took me by surprise. Through reflection, I later recognized that he would not have been comfortable doing so, as it would have meant making himself vulnerable to his students. I do recall the first time that I sat at the front of the room with my eyes closed, and it was rather nerve wracking, but I pushed through the fear and just did it. What I realized after my conversation with that colleague was that I was comfortable being vulnerable with my students. I also became aware of the fact that many teachers do not have that same level of comfort or capacity for being vulnerable, particularly in academia.

During preservice teacher education, conversations frequently turn to the topic of "maintaining control" of the class. William Glasser's (1999) choice theory is based on the concept that every human needs a degree of control and agency in their life. Even prison populations have reduced incidences of violence when prisoners are given minimal choices. The question then, is why do we feel that we have to control students? Why do we not want students to have their own power?

Vulnerability is not about being weak, but conversely is about being genuine and strong. Instead of engaging in ego battles with students, in which no one really "wins," through developing healthy relationships with them, everyone benefits. It is about engaging with students as people rather than subordinates that we must control. As they come to know that we care and are interested in who they are, power struggles can begin to diminish in the classroom. What this requires of us is a willingness and an ability to examine and release our perception of control. In reality we cannot control another human, but we have been conditioned through our own schooling to believe that we need to have control of the students in our classrooms. Losing control of the class is a primary concern that teachers often express.

Challenging Behaviors

On one occasion while I was teaching early years, I attended the end of the year meeting in which teachers were given their class lists for the following year. Information was shared regarding specific students that teachers would be receiving, including some of their needs and challenges. I was informed that I would be receiving a student whom his previous teachers found challenging on many levels. Initially I wondered how I would be able to enjoy my summer holiday thinking about having such a challenging student in the fall. I decided to release that fear and deal with it once school began in September.

The first day of school arrived and I finally met this student. He was slight in stature, had a lot of physical energy, and looked ready for fight or flight. As I soon determined that some of his behaviors were indeed challenging, I decided to engage him on a daily basis to get a better sense of who he was and what he was interested in. I quickly discovered that he needed to feel special, and loved to be asked to do specific tasks, so on a daily basis I gave him special jobs to do such as taking the attendance to the office or helping another student with their reading. This gave him a sense of pride in doing something well.

I also collaborated with him to create a list of things that he could do when he began to notice that he was feeling angry. We placed this list on his desk and when I observed that he was building up tension, I referred him to the list. As he became more aware of himself and the feelings in his body when he became angry, he also began using the strategies independently with increasing levels of success. He still had issues on occasion, but as I gave him more power in the classroom, his behavioral outbursts diminished, and we all made it through the year fairly unscathed. Had I been overly assertive with him and demanded that he follow my orders, I suspect the outcome would have been quite different.

In teaching in a postsecondary setting, I recall having a student who had been "recommended" to my class as he was not fitting into another class. He was a large man who very well could have intimidated most people (I stand just under five feet). When he arrived in my class it was evident that he would not fit comfortably into a standard desk with an attached chair, so in order to accommodate him I ordered a larger table and chair for him. Within a few classes it was evident that he did not possess positive social skills and had difficulty with controlling his impulse to speak. Initially I acknowledged him as he had a wealth of knowledge and I called upon him for responses. It soon became evident that he was going to dominate the class if I allowed him to. I asked him to meet with me and during our discussion about this issue I acknowledged his expertise in particular areas and let him know that all students in the class had a right to equal participation. We came to an agreement that he would self-regulate and try to only speak twice in every class, that he had to become more aware of his need to interject at inappropriate times, and that if he did so, we would have another discussion to brainstorm alternative strategies. Things worked out well and we developed a good working relationship. I did not "play" teacher with this student and exert my power, but rather had honest communications with him. I made myself somewhat vulnerable in the situation.

Fear

What contributes to a teacher's hesitancy to be vulnerable with their students is fear. This includes the fear of not being respected, the fear of students not listening to them or following their instructions, the fear of colleagues viewing them as being too soft, the fear of losing control, and the fear of losing identity, which can be wrapped up in their ideas. Palmer (1998b) addresses the fear that not only lives in the hearts of teachers, but also in the hearts of students in a poignant way:

> From grade school on, education is a fearful enterprise. As a student, I was in too many classrooms riddled with fear, the fear that leads many children, born with a love of learning, to hate the idea of school. As a teacher, I am at my worst when fear takes the lead in me, whether that means teaching in fear of my students or manipulating their fears of me. Our relations as faculty colleagues are often diminished by fear; fear is nearly universal in the relations of faculty and administration; and fear is a standard management tool in too many administrative kit bags. (p. 36)

Current education systems still hold remnants of the beginnings of formalized schooling, which were based on industrial, military, and penal models; hence the image of the teacher having supreme control and power in the classroom remains. The entire structure is rooted in a position of fear. Palmer (1998b) describes the root of our fear:

> We collaborate with the structures of separation because they promise to protect us against one of the deepest fears at the heart of being human—the fear of having a live encounter with alien "otherness," whether the other is a student, a colleague, a subject, or a self-dissenting voice within. We fear encounters in which the other is free to be itself, to speak its own truth, to tell us what we may not wish to hear. We want those encounters on our own terms, so that we can control their outcomes, so that they will not threaten our view of world and self. (p. 37)

This is a profound insight, and at times it can feel much easier and less stressful to hide behind our podiums, course content, and titles. The fear of having a live encounter with another may also be exacerbated in today's culture as more people communicate behind the safety of their electronic devices. The reality is that we can only know the fear in our students when we recognize the fear within ourselves.

Facing Our Fears

Palmer (1998b) goes to the heart of the matter regarding our fear of having a live encounter with a person or people whose responses we cannot predict. It is in essence like live performance and improvisation in theatre. Although actors usually rehearse lines in a script, at times an actor might leave their script and improvise, either due to forgetting their lines or having a moment of inspiration that carries them. This then demands that the other actor or actors have to improvise and go along with their fellow actor in ensuring that the scene carries on following the plot. Master teachers are improvisors of the highest order, as they continually work with student responses and questions, all the while keeping the learning experience flowing and focused.

In order for us to create spaces in which the fear is minimized for our students, we have to examine the fear within our own hearts. At what moments in the classroom do we feel afraid? Can we identify what the root of our fear is? How do we manage and respond to our fear? Can we feel fear without becoming the fear? This kind of exploration can create profound shifts in our perceptions of ourselves and our students, when led by a skilled facilitator. Although this is an experience that every educator is faced with, (and some on a daily basis), I am sure that most have not had an opportunity to explore the many facets of fear in their work.

Through continued work on our inner lives it is possible to become more comfortable with difficult situations in the classroom, and Palmer (1983) illuminates, "Creating a learning space that is not closed down by fearful emotions requires a teacher who is not afraid of feelings" (p. 84). This requires that teachers not only work on their personal development but also have professional opportunities in which to explore and discuss their fears.

The only book that is on the required reading list for my course is Parker J. Palmer's (1998b) book *The Courage to Teach: Exploring the Inner Landscape of a Teacher's Life*. It continues to be one of the most influential books I have read on education, and due to a professor using it in his course, I completed my Master of Education degree in the postsecondary education stream. Although written for in-service teachers, I have found this book to be an excellent starting point for discussions with students regarding their perceptions, beliefs, and experiences as preservice teachers and students. During the course of the year we discuss several chapters from the book, and these sessions contribute to further developing and deepening our learning community.

At the beginning of the first discussion based on this book, I ask my students to sit in chairs in a circle, as this creates a space of equality. I then describe some of the guidelines that Palmer (1999) includes in his guidebook, *The Courage to Teach Guide for Reflection & Renewal*. These include respecting confidentiality so that everyone feels free to express their ideas and opinions safely, and when listening to the speaker to refrain from interjecting with questions or advice. The purpose of these discussions is for students to have a safe space in which they can speak their truth and be heard. As I observe students during these discussions, I become aware that for some of them, this may be one of the only places in which they have an opportunity to freely express themselves and to share the things that are most important to them.

The second discussion of the year revolves around the chapter on fear within both teachers and students, and it is often one of the most powerful experiences we have together. We sit in a circle and I let them know that in this particular session they will put all of their fears about teaching into the middle of the circle. They begin by sharing their fears as teachers, as my students have already spent 5 or 6 weeks in their practicum placements, so have started to get a feel for what their particular classroom ethos is and the challenges that their cooperating teacher faces. As they share the fears that they have as teachers my students begin to realize that they are not alone, and that their peers have similar fears regarding the teaching profession. Many of these fears revolve around challenging student behaviors, the fear that their students will not understand what they are teaching them, the moments when a student asks them a question that they cannot readily answer, and in moments of silence when students do not respond to a question that they ask.

The discussion then turns to the fears that they have as students. This is also illuminating, as my students share their fears of not understanding an assignment and being too shy to ask the teacher for help, being hesitant to answer a question for fear of giving an incorrect response and appearing foolish, not keeping up with their readings, and the fear of judgement by the teacher in the form of receiving a low grade or failing.

During these discussions and others during the course of the year, I also share my experiences with my students, including times that were challenging and activities that I did with students that were not as successful as I had hoped they would be. I find that this has a positive impact on my students. First, it normalizes their experiences, as they hear from their peers and a seasoned teacher who also has fears and who experienced challenges in her teaching. Second, it gives them an opportunity to see me as a human and an ally, rather than exclusively as a teacher. Schoem et al. (2017) support this: "My teaching, the students' learning, and our classroom experience are all greatly enhanced by embracing the humanity that is in me and in my students and is alive in the classroom and by developing the rich human relationships of learning that await" (p. 79).

I recognize and respect that there is a range in the degree to which teachers feel comfortable being vulnerable with their students. Many teachers may not have had a teacher who was vulnerable with them, and this disposition is not often modelled or addressed in preservice teacher education programs, so most teachers have no basis from which to ease into this way of being with students. Some teachers have a natural capacity for vulnerability, whereas others who do not, may choose to develop it. This capacity to be aware of our fears and to face them and continue to engage authentically with students can be developed, and preservice teacher programs are the ideal context in which to begin this exploration.

I believe that one of the reasons that Parker Palmer's (1998b) book, *The Courage to Teach,* has been so well received is that he was the first academic to make himself publicly vulnerable through his writing regarding his inner life as a teacher. His candid writing gave others permission to begin discussing their own fears and challenges with other teachers. Palmer also instituted the Centre for Teacher Renewal, through which thousands of teachers have been provided opportunities to meet with other educators to openly discuss their experiences. Our students expect that we will have expertise in our subject areas, that we will have facility in teaching, and also that we will be genuine human beings.

Kessler (2000) describes, "To be vulnerable is to be willing to feel deeply, to be moved by what a student expresses or by what comes up inside ourselves in the presence of our students or the issues they raise" (p. 121). I have had moments of joy and moments in which I have been moved to tears by the students that I work with. Several years ago, prior to going to work, I received a phone call from my father to inform me that my stepbrother had died of a massive heart attack. Although I was in total shock, I drove to work. I was in my office prior to going to my classroom when I received a message from my husband to let me know that my uncle, who had been very ill, had also just died. I proceeded to my classroom in a total daze and before beginning to teach, I briefly let my students know what had transpired. Many of them expressed their condolences to me and some of them hugged me in an effort to comfort me. During the next few weeks I received sympathy cards from students and was aware that they had empathy for my grief. This most likely would not have occurred had I not shown vulnerability to them throughout the year and in that particularly difficult moment.

Dissipating Fear

There are many things that we can do to dissipate and minimize the fear that our students experience. Being genuine and real with students is crucial, as they begin to view us as humans rather than solely as authority figures. For some who "play the role" of teacher, it is as though there exists a pane of glass between them and their students. They share information but often do not reveal themselves or encourage interaction, so in essence there is a barrier between them and their students, and relationship is minimal. For one who is genuine and who shares their true self with their students, the barrier dissolves and deeper interactions begin to occur, leading to relationship. Thus, the students begin to see us in a different light; that of human and teacher.

Using humor in the classroom can be very effective in dissipating fear, as it minimizes tension and contributes to the creation of a relaxed learning environment. Students cannot learn in an environment in which there is high pressure, limited time to work on assignments, and fear of being judged by the teacher. Humor creates a light-heartedness, and when people laugh together, they feel better.

Our selection of assignments also affects the degree of fear that students feel in our classrooms. When students are given opportunities to make choices in some of their learning, they have agency, knowing that their teacher is supporting their choices rather than dictating all of them. The only assignments that I remember from my schooling were those in which I chose the topic and the mode of representation.

Assessment practices also contribute to lowering the barriers between teachers and students, as grades are a form of judgement from an authority figure. Constructive feedback on assignments provides students with important information regarding their work, including what they need to work on in order to progress in their learning. Putting a C– on an assignment with no form of feedback often feels like harsh judgement on the part of students. Self-assessment is one form of assessment that engages the students in creating criteria for quality work and monitoring the progress of their work. When my students use self-assessment for an inquiry and peer teaching assignment, some of them report that knowing that I was not assessing them took the pressure off of them and gave them greater freedom in taking risks in their learning.

Creating a learning environment in which students feel that they belong and where their voice is honored without retribution is a key component to reducing fear. When a student knows that their responses will be met with sarcasm, anger, humiliation, or intimidation, they will understandably be highly unlikely to engage in classroom activities. The outdated mode of autocratic teaching in which the teacher has supreme authority over the students was not effective in the past, and certainly does not work today. Having students fall in line and follow all of the teacher's directives was based on military and penal models, and was hardly an effective model for working with children and youth. A student will comply when they are afraid of their teacher but will not learn much other than what it feels like to be afraid of an adult in authority.

All of these practices have the effect of levelling the power structure within the classroom. When students have voice and choice in the classroom and know that their teacher genuinely wants them to have power, the entire dynamic of the classroom shifts and becomes more enlivened.

Dissipating and minimizing the fear that we feel in the classroom can occur in several ways. As we work on our inner lives through reading, seeking counsel, and reflection, and as we develop the capacity to feel and face fear in our personal lives, the better equipped we are to handle those moments of fear in the classroom. This inner work translates to our work with our students. As we begin to recognize moments when we are afraid, and then choose how to respond rather than react, we can gradually change our relationship to fear. Having discussions with trusted colleagues and attending professional development sessions can also better equip us to handle difficult moments in the classroom.

Palmer (1998b) reveals:

> Each time I walk into a classroom, I can choose the place within myself from which my teaching will come, just as I can choose the place within my students toward which my teaching will be aimed. I need not teach from a fearful place: I can teach from curiosity or hope or empathy or honesty, places that are as real within me as are my fears. I can have fear, but I need not be fear—if I am willing to stand someplace else in my inner landscape. (p. 57)

Kessler (2000) shares that

> it takes courage for teachers to work with students at the level of heart and soul. Entering this arena . . . can drop us into the cauldron of our own emotional and spiritual growth. But the rewards are great for teachers who are willing to engage their own depths, meeting the demons and the allies that dwell within. (p. 126)

It is imperative to create communities of learners in which all involved feel safe and cared for enough for most of the fear that they feel to drop away, to enable them to fully engage their learning. It is important to create spaces where people can be vulnerable with each other and where people can freely be who they are. Alderfer (2015) speaks to this: "In touching our students' lives from the warmhearted core of who we are, we can become true peacemakers" (p. xxxi). My experience has revealed to me that as I allow myself to be real and vulnerable with my students, that our relationships become deeper, as does our community and our learning. I recognize that in doing so, I also give my students permission to engage their vulnerability and to be real.

5

The Seed

One of the deepest longings of the human soul is to be seen.
—John O'Donohue (1999)

The Inner Lives of Teachers and Students

We live in an era in which materialism, productivity, and multitasking are revered. What this means is that a focus on one's inner life can often be ignored or negated, as the pressure to meet external demands is omnipresent. With an emphasis on covering the mandated curriculum and preparing students for standardized tests, many teachers feel the pressure of meeting these demands in their work. As students and teachers alike enter their classrooms as whole human beings, they also bring their inner self, which naturally requires engagement and expression.

This chapter reaches the center of the spiral and focuses on the importance of incorporating teachers' and students' inner lives into their work. It commences with three educational positions or approaches to teaching, a brief description of one of the ways in which I invite students to bring their inner life into the classroom, followed by an exploration of spirituality as

Flourishing in the Holistic Classroom, pages 83–103
Copyright © 2021 by Information Age Publishing
All rights of reproduction in any form reserved.

it pertains to preservice teacher education. Inviting, encouraging, and supporting students to connect their inner self or soul to their work has the capacity for cultivating a core feature of flourishing, which is self-esteem. It also provides the conditions in which learners can develop the additional features of flourishing, which are vitality and optimism, as they connect with their inner needs and desires.

Holistic education is concerned with educating students from the totality of their being—spirit, mind, and body. Chapman and McClendon (2018) describe:

> Taking inner realities seriously means taking individuals and their values seriously. It means recognizing that learning and making sense involves the personal (Dirkx, Mezirow, & Cranton, 2006)—the subjective. It means giving attention to personal questions about the meaning of life, of chosen work, of relationships, of what matters and why these things matter. Focusing on inner realities is educative because it calls into question and brings into focus personal authenticity and integrity. (p. 11)

Inviting and encouraging students to investigate and explore things that matter to them has the potential to help a student who is apathetic about meeting mandated learning outcomes, come to life in the classroom. If we want citizens to attend to those things that they care about in their lives, surely public education is a prime place for this kind of exploration to begin. If we want students to care about learning, we must provide them with opportunities to discover what they care deeply about through connecting with their inner self or soul.

The spiritual aspect is important, as we are spiritual beings whether we acknowledge that we are or not. By being spiritual, I am not implying being religious, however many people who identify with a religion also say that they have a spiritual life, while others do not. The spiritual dimension of education is concerned with the inner spark, the essence, or soul of the person, and how that interacts with others, the Earth, and beyond. Nava (2001) notes, "Spirituality refers to a living force within us, to our most profound and real nature" (p. 129). Lantieri (2001) states, "Spiritual experience can be described as the conscious recognition of a connection that goes beyond our minds or emotions" (p. 8). In this way, we are inviting students to engage their learning from the center of their being.

What is happening interiorly for students is important, and it is critical for them to have opportunities to bring their inner life to their learning experiences, in order to make deeper connections and create relevance. In nature, all growth occurs from the inside out and children likewise have an inner impulse towards growth and learning. They are innately curious, and without prompting from an adult they explore their world with curiosity, purpose, and enthusiasm. As Crowell and Reid-Marr (2013) note:

> A spiritual focus is an important consideration in teaching the whole person. It means *breathing life* into the curriculum and infusing the learning process with the wonder and awe of content, with the joy of living and the significance of possibility. It connects the external and internal worlds as natural partners in the search for meaning and incorporates imagination and creativity as essential characteristics of life's journey. (p. 124)

Binder (2011) addresses spiritual literacy in the classroom:

> While other domains of development are important, including spirituality deepens growth at levels not often discussed or embraced in the classroom: children's interconnectedness to self, others and the world. Nurturing the core of children's inner landscapes provides the still spaces needed to connect to their experiences, the non-judgmental breadth to explore their feelings and the mindful presence to understand what is meaningful. (p. 32)

Holistic Curriculum

J. Miller (2007) describes the three key principles of holistic education as balance, inclusion, and connection. As mentioned previously, the three educational orientations or positions that J. Miller (2007) puts forth as being inclusive are transmission, transaction, and transformation. Teaching from a position of transmission means that there is a one-way transmission of information, process, or a skill directly from the teacher to the students, similar to how a radio transmits a message. The teacher is viewed as the donor of knowledge and the students receive the information. An example is when a teacher recites information about a particular topic such as molecules, and the students listen and write down notes. As J. Miller (2007) describes, "Knowledge is seen as fixed rather than as a process, and is usually broken down into smaller units so that students can master the material" (p. 10).

The transaction position can be likened to any kind of transaction that you engage in. For example, when you conduct a sales transaction you trade money for goods or services. In the classroom, this interaction is often a two-way dialogue, in which the teacher initiates questions or problems for students to solve and the students are invited to respond or ask questions of the teacher or their peers. J. Miller (2007) states, "However, this dialogue stresses cognitive interactions since analysis is stressed more than synthesis and thinking more than feeling" (p. 11).

The transformation position includes the curriculum and the child, thus as J. Miller (2007) notes, "The aim of the transformation position is the development of the whole person. The student is not reduced to a set of learning competencies or thinking skills but is seen as a whole being" (p. 11). Examples of strategies used include guided visualization, engagement with the arts, and cooperative learning. The transformation position is inclusive, in that it incorporates transmission and transaction. Students are encouraged to bring their inner self to their learning, thus making connections and creating relevance.

In the course that I teach I spend two classes introducing my students to the positions of transmission, transaction, and transformation as the inclusion of all of these approaches reflects holistic pedagogy (J. Miller, 2007).

When I teach the class on transmissive and transactional teaching, I use each specific approach to model it to my students. At the beginning of the first class I invite a student who I had previously asked, to recite the "To Be or Not to Be" soliloquy from Shakespeare's play Hamlet. This dramatic way of beginning a class definitely garners students' attention. I then proceed to teach them about transmissive teaching using a PowerPoint presentation, and I speak very quickly and do not ask questions or allow my students to ask questions. After I am finished, I ask them the following questions: "What did I do?"; "What did you do?"; and "How did you feel?" This proves to be poignant, as they quickly realize that I modeled transmissive teaching to them. I then return to the beginning of the PowerPoint presentation and go through the aims, strategies, and forms of assessment inherent in transmissive teaching. We then have a discussion regarding when it is appropriate to use the transmissive approach, as well as the benefits and challenges of it. I conclude by asking them how they would teach Hamlet in a transmissive way, including what the teacher and students would do.

When teaching them about transactional teaching I slow the pace down, ask my students questions, ask them to discuss a topic with a partner, and allow room for them to ask questions during the session. I then ask them the same questions that I posed to them for transmissive teaching: "What did I do?" "What did you do?" "How did you feel?" Once again, I go over the aims, strategies, and forms of assessment for transactional teaching, followed by discussing when using the position of transaction is appropriate and what the benefits and challenges of it are. I then ask them how they would teach Hamlet in a transactional way, including what the teacher and students would specifically do. I find this approach to be a very dramatic and effective way of demonstrating each approach, as students learn about them experientially.

During the next class I model transformative teaching by taking them through a guided visualization. First, I explain the entire process to them in order to make them less apprehensive, and in particular, I let them know that not everyone can readily visualize. If visualization is unfamiliar or difficult for them, I invite them to use their other senses to connect with the experience. Kinesthetic learners may feel something during the experience, while others may hear or smell something. This can reduce the stress levels of some students who find visualization challenging. I then take them through a guided visualization that gradually leads them to getting in touch with their dream of becoming a teacher. They engage all of their senses in imagining that they are in their ideal classroom. I ask them to imagine where they are, who is there with them, what sounds they hear, as well as anything that they feel or smell. I encourage them to be in touch with the feelings that they have being in that space with their students.

Holding onto that feeling and using all of their other senses, in silence, they then go to the table and select a color of construction paper they are attracted to, along with several colors of pastels. I invite them to express the special feeling that they had visually, and I let them know that they do not have to draw images, but rather to allow the colors and the way that they apply the pastels onto the paper, to express that particular feeling. They may also use markers to write words on the paper. They engage in this activity remaining silent, to ensure that they are staying in touch with the feeling that they had during the guided visualization.

After everyone has finished, I invite them to comment on the process and the experience. Some students find it refreshing to have an opportunity to engage their inner world and imagination, and to express their understandings in a manner other than written form. At times students have shared that it was a very deep experience for them or that the result was a total surprise to them. Others share that they had some degree of reluctance and fear, as they had not created visual art since they were in elementary school.

What is revealed in this exercise is that students often make connections through the guided visualization and visual art in more powerful ways than they would have through written form. This exercise demonstrates the importance of providing students with opportunities to engage their imagination and inner self or soul, and to then express their experience in an alternative mode. I ask them the same questions; share the aims, strategies, and forms of assessment regarding the position of transformation; followed by a discussion on the inherent benefits and challenges. Finally, I ask them how they would teach Hamlet in a transformative way, including what the teacher and students would specifically do.

Holistic educators understand the importance of soul work and provide their students with regular opportunities in which to engage their inner self in their academic work. All humans experience moments of insight, clarity, and perhaps a totally new way of perceiving a concept. This is how new theories and inventions are birthed. Likewise, our students can experience powerful insights while sitting in our classrooms as we teach them about molecules, poetry, geometry, or watercolor painting. The question is, "Do we provide them with regular opportunities to work with their insights?" "Do we create space and time for them to express and share their ideas, or do we plough ahead with our agenda and information?" These are key questions that holistic educators ponder, as they are very aware that their students' inner lives are a key component in the learning process.

Chapman and McClendon (2018) speak to transformation:

> According to John Dirkx (1998), learning *is* soul work. Soul work is the transformative learning that comes from a focus on our subjectivity, on the nature of the self, and on the various ways we understand our senses of self and identify. Soul work involves integrating the deeply personal intellectual, emotional, moral, and spiritual dimensions of our being in the world. (p. 12)

There are many ways that we can invite students to engage and express their inner world in their academic work. Some examples include asking them to write their opinions on a variety of topics, creating a piece of art to express their understanding of a theme from a book or play, choreographing a dance or creating a series of tableaux to illustrate adaptations in plants, or writing journal entries from a particular character's perspective in a novel. If we want students to engage their learning and to create relevance, we must invite and encourage them to engage from their deepest self.

The arts in particular are very conducive to providing students with nontraditional and multimodal ways of expressing their learning, and for connecting with their inner self or soul in powerful ways. When one has a deep understanding or knowing that may be difficult to express in aural or written form, creating a sculpture, choreographing a dance, or composing a piece of music may be the most effective and visceral way of communicating to others. Cornett (1999) supports this, "From their earliest beginnings, humans have been compelled to express ideas and feelings through the arts. Thirty thousand years ago paintings were made on a cave wall in southern France (Chauvet et al., 1996)" (p. 3). Each art form is a unique language and thus, choosing a particular form may be most appropriate to express a specific understanding or knowing. The proficiency that the student has with an art form will also dictate which form they may choose.

Providing students with opportunities to choose their medium of expression for assignments can often result in a more in-depth representation of their understanding of a concept or idea, and they can also become more engaged in the learning process. Cornett (1999) highlights the importance of the arts in education, "Arts specialists have long known that the arts offer a distinct means for meaning making..." (p. 4).

The experience of many students reads as follows: In the early years they are given opportunities to play, explore, and experiment on a daily basis. Upon entering Grades 3 or 4, these opportunities often wane, and by the time they are in senior years their learning consists of memorizing facts and regurgitating them on tests or writing essays or papers. Many students are rarely given assignments that allow them to explore a concept by connecting to their inner world. This is particularly problematic for students in middle or senior years, as they are experimenting with issues of identity, belonging, and purpose in life. What is also problematic about not providing students with opportunities for contemplation and reflection is that they can readily become robots—waking up, going to school or work, going home, doing chores—in essence being on a hamster wheel. It is not until a person has an opportunity to introspect that they have the time and space in which transformation and new choices can emerge.

This has been validated for me on a regular basis when I introduce the inquiry and peer teaching assignment to my students. I ask them if they have ever done an inquiry project and fewer than 2% of them report that they have. One rationale for giving them this assignment is for them to experience what learning feels like when they drive the entire process from selecting a topic, to researching it, expressing their learning in a mode of representation that they choose, and finally assessing themselves based on criteria that they determine. It is so unfortunate that they have experienced 16 or more years of schooling and have rarely had such an opportunity.

One of my objectives as an instructor in a preservice teacher education program is to model ways of providing students with opportunities to engage their learning from their inner self. If they are invited and encouraged to engage their learning from the level of soul, deep transformation is possible for them. A term that can be used to describe one's inner self and how it is connected to others and the world around them is spirituality. The following section addresses the spiritual dimension in the context of preservice teacher education.

Quest for Wholeness: Spirituality in Preservice Teacher Education

The word "spirituality" can evoke intense interest from some people, and cause others to become defensive or physically recoil. Despite the charged nature of the word "spirituality," what is occurring on university campuses is the recognition that the spiritual dimension can contribute to learning in meaningful ways, and Scott (1990) asserts that what is called for is "our evolution toward a more integrative definition of knowledge, practice of research, and facilitation of student learning" (p. 16). Although the Latin root of university is *universus,* meaning "whole" or "one," suggesting a holistic paradigm for teaching and learning in postsecondary institutions, the dominant paradigm does not reflect this. As professors and students alike engage in learning, the dominant focus is often objectivism and reductionism in both research and teaching, and as Palmer (1998b) argues, "Although the academy claims to value multiple modes of knowing, it honors only one—an "objective" way of knowing that takes us into the "real" world by taking us "out of ourselves" (p. 17). One wonders how one can come to fully understand a subject or a concept if one is metaphorically disembodied.

What is evident on university campuses is a paradigm shift from instruction, to teaching and learning, with the goal of producing learning (Barr & Tagg, 1995). The acknowledgement of the spiritual dimension in teaching and learning in the postsecondary context can contribute to honoring alternative ways of knowing, by allowing students and teachers to engage the "real" world while remaining connected to their inner lives or "real" world; thus remembering themselves.

This writing supports the argument for acknowledging and honoring the spiritual dimension in teacher education programs for students and professors, as a means of providing opportunities for all to engage their subject matter, the world, their peers, and themselves in an integrative, holistic manner. A definition of spirituality is offered, along with its role in relation to religion (Kessler, 2000; Lantieri, 2001; J. Miller, 2000; Palmer, 1998b), as it can be argued that to be human is to be spiritual and that spirituality is an inherent human characteristic. The role of spirituality in the context of postsecondary education is then discussed (Chickering et al., 2006; Palmer, 2003; Scott, 1990; Tisdell, 2003). In particular, the inclusion of spirituality in teacher education is examined, highlighting the importance of providing a balance to the externally focused approaches that current educational practices embody.

The acknowledgement of the spiritual dimension in teacher education programs has the potential to demonstrate how the intellect can be joined with heart and soul, which will contribute to teachers in training who are not only equipped with methods and theories, but also self-knowledge (Palmer, 2003). It concludes with implications for acknowledging and honoring the spiritual dimension in teacher education programs.

I decided to become a teacher over 30 years ago based on my desire to assist children in developing their full potential. I intuited on a deep level that the inner lives of the children that I worked with were important, and that it was incumbent upon me to provide them with opportunities to engage their inner as well as their outer lives. The growth of the child's inner life or soul can be compared to their physical growth, both of which are dependent on being fed and nurtured, and when young people are given opportunities to explore and express their spirituality, they thrive (Kessler, 2000). I experienced great joy in working with children in Grades 1, 2, and 3, through observing their innate curiosity and freedom in exploring the world around them. I understood that they arrived at school each day as whole human beings; mind, body, and spirit, and often with deep questions. What a lot of children soon begin to learn from the messages that they receive from the adults entrusted with their care is that these deep questions are not acknowledged or honored in the place called school.

This acknowledgment of the spiritual dimension is an integral part of my pedagogy which is grounded in holistic education. Holistic education is founded on the principle of wholeness, and as R. Miller describes in his interview with Koegel (2003), "Holistic education focuses on meaning, connection, and the search for wholeness" (p. 14).

Spirituality and Religion

During any discussion on the topic of spirituality, the question of whether or not one is talking about religion is inevitably raised. Researchers approach the relation of spirituality to religion in numerous ways, including making a clear distinction between the two and describing ways in which they overlap. Many authors make a clear distinction between spirituality and religion (Chickering et al., 2006; Nash, 2001; Tisdell, 2003), differentiating between religion as following a religious tradition and spirituality focusing on an inner journey of growth (Chickering et al., 2006). The distinction between an institutional structure and an individual experience is also noted, as Tisdell (2003) emphasizes, "Organizational religions have institutionalized components to them—written doctrine, codes of regulatory behavior, and organized communities of faith. Spirituality is more about how people make meaning through experience of wholeness, a perceived higher power, or higher purpose" (p. 47). Those who differentiate between spirituality and religion regard spirituality as being more personal and experiential, as contrasted with religion, which is institutional, public, and dogmatic. Bainbridge's (2000) study of 1,195 intending teachers, which was comprised of an open-ended questionnaire regarding their ideas on spirituality, revealed that most respondents made a distinction between religion and spirituality.

Other authors believe that spirituality and religion can be interrelated (Kessler, 2000; Nash, 2001; Webster, 2004), as Nash (2001) illustrates:

> I believe the two terms actually represent two closely related perspectives—the institutional and the personal—on the same phenomenon, transcendence. In my usage, religion is what we do with others, spirituality is what we do within ourselves; the former is public faith, the latter is private faith. (p. 7)

There are people who identify themselves as being religious, yet do not belong to a religious institution, and those who engage in a spiritual practice with others.

As spirituality is discussed in a postmodern context, where various academic disciplines continue to view it through a modern lens, confusion is bound to arise. In response to this confusion some researchers are offering a new postmodern lens through which to look at spirituality, and indeed they are describing it as a postmodern spirituality with new frameworks and language (Tacey, 2002). Tacey (2002) describes how postmodern processes and valuation of uncertainty have contributed to transforming modern assumptions, but that due to the deep secularism of academia, spirituality and religion have not been transformed in the same way, and Tacey (2002) states that in fact "the deconstruction of religion in theology has not, or not yet, had much impact on how religion and spirituality are viewed in the mainstream disciplines of sociology, history, philosophy, literature, or cultural studies" (p. 173). What is important to note at this juncture, is that fruitful, engaging dialogues regarding spirituality can only truly begin when common language is developed. Only then can the paradigm shift begin to happen.

If engaging one's spirituality within educational settings can provide students with deep, integrative understandings of themselves, others, their subject areas, and the greater world, then why is it excluded from most postsecondary educational environments?

Characteristics of Spirituality

Arriving at a definition of spirituality is somewhat like trying to describe love; one feels or knows what it is, yet articulating it is problematic at best. Due to its highly subjective nature, trying to define spirituality is complex, and although there are inherent difficulties in arriving at consensus regarding a definition of spirituality, there are some common characteristics of spirituality that many authors identify. The main characteristics of spirituality that are identified in the literature include: (a) search for meaning/ search for meaning and purpose; (b) relatedness, connectedness, and interconnectedness; (c) relationship to a higher power; (d) sacredness; (e) transcendence; and (f) self-knowledge.

Upon reviewing the literature on spirituality in education, the search for meaning was consistently identified as a central characteristic by the majority of authors (Kessler, 2000; J. Miller, 2006). Creating meaning from one's existence is of central importance to students in postsecondary institutions, as they are at pivotal points in their lives, often making the transition from late adolescence into adulthood. Most authors concurred, adding the element of search for purpose to the search for meaning (Fraser, 2004; Love & Talbot, 1999; McGee, Nagel, & Moore, 2003; V. M. Miller, 2001; Rolph, 1991). Many students in college or university are at a key period of spiritual development in which they are more fully discovering their identity and attempting to make meaning of their lives.

The second characteristic of spirituality as reported by numerous researchers is relatedness, connectedness and interconnectedness of self, others, and a higher power (Chávez, 2001; Harvey, 2004; Kessler, 2000; Lantieri, 2001; J. Miller, 2018; Yasuno, 2004). Their assertion of the importance of relatedness is key, as humans are relational beings who depend on healthy connections with others, often for their very survival. Young people in particular desperately want to be seen and heard (Kessler, 2000), highlighting the need for educators to facilitate the development of healthy relationships within their learning communities. If schools are to become healthy communities of learners, the foundation must be the development and nurturing of healthy relationships.

The importance of a connection to a higher power is noted, as the findings of the UCLA study on the spiritual life of students revealed that three-quarters of students expressed that they experienced a connection to something greater than themselves (Lindholm, 2005). Although the reference to a higher power or God is not consistently evident in the literature, studies such as that administered by UCLA indicate that some students do identify with a presence or entity beyond themselves. What is not clear is how students define God or a higher power. The centrality of the connection between self, others, and a higher power illustrates the innate human drive for connectedness.

The levels of interconnectedness as identified by the authors ranges from that between humans and a divine source, to that between humans and others, to a complete web of all beings including a higher power or God. I propose that the interconnections between all things exist, and quantum physicists have proven this, but that what is important is the person's level of conscious awareness of these connections.

Third, the importance that students placed on their relationship to a higher power as being separate from connection to self or others was reported; some researchers did not include relationship to a higher power with relationship to self and others (Chickering et al., 2006; de Souza & Watson, 2016; Ruiz, 2005). Although not all students identify a connection to a higher power as being important to them, the feeling that one is connected to something outside of and beyond one's self can provide an anchor for many students.

Fourth, several authors identified sacredness as being a central characteristic of spirituality (Chickering et al., 2006; Palmer, 1998b). What people identify as being sacred is personal, from having an experience in nature, reading a particular text, or observing a piece of art. In essence, the sacred is found in whatever a person deems being worthy of respect. In educational settings, acknowledging the sacred can add richness, depth, and relevance to students' learning experiences.

The fifth characteristic of spirituality found in the review of the literature is transcendence (Duff, 2003; McGee, Nagel & Moore, 2003; J. Miller, 2018). The feelings associated with rising above one's normal mode of being, or of going beyond the boundaries of self are common themes in the literature on spirituality in education. People sometimes refer to experiences of transcendence as "aha moments" when connectedness, clarity, or insight occurs.

The final characteristic of spirituality as gleaned from the review of the literature is self-knowledge (De Souza, 2003; Duff, 2003; Fraser, 2004; Krishnamurti, 1977). Through discovering and coming to know one's self, one is better able to relate to others and the world, and Krishnamurti (1977) believed that "ignorance is not the lack of knowledge but of self-knowing; without self-knowing there is no intelligence" (p. 97). In the context of education, this has implications for teachers and administrators in providing a balance to exteriorly imposed knowledge. Throughout the literature review on spirituality in education, I consistently noted a characteristic that was minimally represented, but which I believe is an intrinsic component of spirituality; a connectedness and interconnectedness to the earth and the cosmos. Some authors noted the connection to the Earth in their descriptions of spirituality (Caine, 2003; Fenwick, English, & Parsons, 2001; Koegel, 2003; J. Miller, 2007), yet these represent a minority.

My rationale for including the connection to the Earth and the cosmos derives from my assertion that it is narcissistic of humans to think that although we inhabit a living, breathing planet, that we are somehow divorced from its very being. Furthermore, we are wired for connection to the earth and the cosmos and as Tucker (1996) describes Thomas Berry's work, "He calls for reinventing the human at the species level which implies moving from our cultural coding to recover our genetic coding of relatedness to the earth" (p. 3). One of the great tragedies of our technological, reductionistic, competitive, and consumeristic society is that this exclusive focus has metaphorically and literally ripped us from the fabric of our very being and our sustenance.

The spiritualities of indigenous peoples including the Maori in New Zealand (Fraser, 2004) and the First Nations peoples of Canada (Wilson & Wilson, 1998) illuminate the connection to the Earth and the cosmos. Fraser (2004) describes the amalgamation of Christian and Maori beliefs in education in New Zealand, including the incorporation of Maori prayers to "*Tangaroa* (God of the sea) and *Papatuanuku* (Earth mother). Relational accountability can be a principle of indigenous peoples' spiritualities, as the interconnectivity of all life is valued and all individual actions are in relation to every living organism and must be honored (Wilson & Wilson, 1998, p. 157). As we reconnect with the Earth and the cosmos, we will begin the process of remembering ourselves and in doing so, create opportunities to remember not only our institutions, but our world.

Based on the research of these scholars the characteristics of spirituality include a search for meaning and purpose, relatedness, connectedness and interconnectedness, a relationship to a higher power, sacredness, transcendence, self-knowledge, as well as my inclusion of a connectedness and interconnectedness to the Earth and the cosmos. These characteristics are not static, but rather take on significance in relation to one's level of awareness.

Check Your Spirit at the Door: Spirituality in Postsecondary Education

Upon entering a recording studio, a sign is usually posted above the door reading "Check ego at door." In a similar way, when professors and students enter their learning environments on a daily basis, they are covertly asked to check their spirits at the door. As a result of educational institutions' efforts to avoid religious indoctrination, on most university campuses there is limited focus on spirituality and religion. Within the context of postsecondary education, the prevalent paradigm is objectivism, which Palmer (1998b) states, "treats the world as an object to be dissected and manipulated, a way of knowing that gives us power over the world" (p. 2). This dualistic epistemology results in teachers and learners feeling disconnected, fragmented, and alienated from not only their studies, but from each other, the world, and ultimately themselves. Vestiges of colonialism are also present in academia, as Shahjahan (2005) states, "such positivist secular discourses are colonial in nature and have a long history of displacing non-dominant ways of knowing the world, especially spiritually" (p. 693). The effects of this exclusion of indigenous knowledges impacts teachers and students, and the academy is being called upon to recognize and validate other ways of knowing (Dei, 2000; Shahjahan, 2005).

The spiritual dimension is absent in most curricula in postsecondary settings, and students become quite adept at both learning and demonstrating their learning in a fragmented manner. This fragmentation of organizational structures in postsecondary education is well documented (J. Miller, 2007; Palmer, 1998b; Scott, 2002; Shahjahan, 2005). If one engages the "real" world by being disconnected from self, perhaps that is what one ultimately comes to know; that learning is fragmented and that as the learner is not in relation to the subject, the learner ultimately does not matter. Although this fear of developing relationships between things and people is threatening to the academy, imagine how much deeper, richer, and complete our levels of understanding our areas of investigation could be if we engaged them with our whole selves.

Although there is often fear associated with acknowledging the spiritual dimension in postsecondary education (Chickering et al., 2005; Palmer, 1998b), it is often more of an issue for the professoriate than for the student body. The findings of UCLA's comprehensive study entitled *Spirituality and the Professoriate: A National Study of Faculty Beliefs, Attitudes, and Behaviors,* which was conducted on some 40,670 faculty at 421 colleges and universities, describe the disparity between what faculty believe and how they teach.

They reported that four in five faculty identified themselves as being spiritual, and that more than two-thirds reported that they purposefully seek out opportunities for spiritual growth. Almost half of those surveyed described the integration of the spiritual dimension in their lives as being essential (Lindholm, 2005b). In order for students to be provided with opportunities in which to engage the spiritual dimension within the context of their academic studies, professors must also be given permission to acknowledge the spiritual dimension in their work.

Spirituality is not typically represented on the campuses of most Canadian universities despite the overwhelming research that indicates that the student body has a deep hunger for the spiritual dimension in their lives (Kessler, 2000; R. Miller, 2001; Scott, 2002). The Higher Education Research Institute (HERI) at the University of California in Los Angeles carried out a study on 112,232 first-year students attending 236 colleges and universities, entitled *The Spiritual Life of College Students: A National Study of College Students' Search for Meaning and Purpose,* in which this spiritual hunger was expressed (Lindholm, 2005a). Eighty percent of the student body reported being interested in spirituality and feeling joy in relation to their spirituality, while half of them indicated that it is very important for them to seek spiritual growth opportunities. Furthermore, 80% of the students surveyed discussed religion/spirituality with others, over 75% of them believe in God, and 48% of the students surveyed expressed an expectation of their colleges and universities to help them develop spiritually (Lindholm, 2005a). As evidenced in the literature review, students place great importance on spirituality, as they find themselves navigating through increasingly complex social issues. The acknowledgement of the spiritual dimension in postsecondary settings has the potential to create holistic institutions.

Spirituality in Teacher Education

"We teach who we are" (Palmer, 1998b, p. 1). Palmer's (1998b) words are powerful and challenge educators to examine their inner lives more closely. If we do teach who we are, what are we modeling for teachers in training? Do we model ways of being in the world that are holistic and integrative or do we continue to adhere to educational approaches that are based on objectivism, reductionism, and fragmentation?

An examination of spirituality in teacher education revealed little support for acknowledging the spiritual dimension in teacher education programs (J. Miller, 2000; Palmer, 2003; Rolph, 1991). The social context of teacher education impacts on expectations of both teachers and learners, often excluding the spiritual dimension. The technological, consumeristic, nature of society focuses on the external, material needs of people, to the detriment of their spiritual needs (Rolph, 1991). This focus on externals results in fragmentation in education as well, and as R. Miller (2001) states:

> Our considerable powers of intellect have served primarily to disconnect us from the world. Modern systems of education have fed these powers well, training young people how to gain knowledge *over* the world, knowledge at the expense of feeling, information without wisdom, facts without moral discernment. (p. 31)

As knowledge becomes a commodity which one wields in the world, rather than something that one comes to deeply know and love, it ultimately breeds dispassion. Yet within this societal context the spiritual dimension is invisibly omnipresent. Spirituality can be likened to the elephant in the middle of the room; everyone is aware of its presence, yet it is ignored, and Palmer (1998a) asserts that spirituality "is at the heart of every subject we teach, where it waits to be brought forth" (p. 8). Although some professors are courageous enough to acknowledge the spiritual dimension in their teaching, many do not. Teachers in training must be prepared to guide students through their deep and sometimes perplexing questions, and this will best be accomplished by developing future teachers who more fully understand their inner lives.

Within conventional educational practices which focus on externally based knowledge, the idea of acknowledging the spiritual dimension in learning may be seen as a threat not only to educators and administrators, but to the very maintenance of the institution. Although there is reluctance to incorporate the spiritual dimension into teacher education programs, many educators do incorporate Gardner's (1993) theory of multiple intelligences and Goleman's (1995) research on emotional intelligence into their classrooms. Gardner has included existential intelligence to his theory and several researchers have identified spiritual intelligence as a separate intelligence (Vaughan, 2002; Zohar & Marshall, 2000).

In light of the research on holistic education and spirituality in education, glimmers of hope exist for the eventual acknowledgement of the spiritual dimension in teacher education programs, providing teachers in training with opportunities to not only acquire solid foundational knowledge and skills, but a deeper understanding of who they are.

Implications

Today educators are faced with a barrage of demands, and as Johnson (2005) argues, "In a world of Praxis exams, No Child Left Behind, standardized achievement tests, behavioral objectives, technical teaching, emotionless pedagogy, and standards-based education it often feels like a holistic philosophy and authentic teaching are not valued" (p. 36). Professors who teach in teacher education programs are no less immune to these expectations, including courses that are mandated by governments and program changes imposed by institutional leadership.

How then, can the spiritual dimension be acknowledged and honored within the context of teacher education? Rogers and Hill (2002) maintain "that topics such as spirituality should be included as an integral part of the curriculum for undergraduate teacher education students" (p. 288). Although I agree with the latter part of their statement, I would not refer to spirituality as a topic to be included in a curriculum, but rather it is a dimension of being human.

I recommend that two broad areas be considered in order to affect a shift from externally imposed educational practices to a balance between the outer and the inner worlds of students and teachers; the institutional level and the individual level. First, the institutional culture must begin to acknowledge other ways of knowing, as an exclusive objectivist epistemology will only result in further fragmentation, and Scott (1990) states that what is called for is "our evolution toward a more integrative definition of knowledge, practice of research, and facilitation of student learning" (p. 16). Indigenous knowledges must be acknowledged and honored as valid modes of knowing, and as Dei (2000) states, "To achieve a genuine synthesis of all existing knowledges, the academy must work with the idea of multiple, collective and collaborative dimensions of knowledge" (p. 119). It is therefore incumbent upon administrators and policy makers to facilitate this paradigm shift towards more integrative, holistic learning.

Teacher education programs have the most inherent power and responsibility to affect the education system and these institutions must support the development of teachers who will be equipped to respond to the spiritual needs of their students (Renteria, 2001). Clearly, teacher educators must be supported by their administrators and each other, to begin to acknowledge the spiritual dimension within the context of their academic work. What is called for is teachers who embody wholeness in their classrooms and as Palmer (1998b) emphasizes,

Teaching and learning, done well, are done not by disembodied intellects but by whole persons whose minds cannot be disconnected from feeling and spirit, from heart and soul. To teach as a whole person to the whole person is not to lose one's professionalism as a teacher but to take it to a deeper level. (p. 10)

Second, although the inclusion of spirituality into postsecondary contexts cannot be mandated by administration, individual professors and instructors can begin to acknowledge their inner lives in their academic work and teach from their wholeness. I am not suggesting that educators jump on yet another "band wagon," but I am inviting them to examine how they might begin to integrate their inner lives with their outer lives in their work.

There are four recommendations that I offer to teachers as they begin acknowledging and honoring the spiritual dimension in their classrooms. First, as all of the identified characteristics of spirituality are about relationship, teachers must purposefully create safe, open and caring environments in which relationships can be developed. Authentic sharing on the part of both the teacher and the students begins to cultivate trust between class members, and in the process, community develops. During various points in my career, at the beginning of each of my classes I incorporated a sharing time in which the students and I shared significant events in our lives. The students became comfortable in their sharing with the class, as they began to realize that it is a safe place to do so. What I often observed as the term progressed was that the level of sharing deepened, and besides recommending good movies to the group, students also began to share significant personal events, both joyful and sometimes quite tragic. This level of sharing not only allowed the students and me to learn more about each other but gave us an opportunity to develop and demonstrate compassion for one another. Although this may seem like a trite activity, it proved to be one of the most powerful strategies that I employed in my teaching. Although, I rarely use the word *spirituality* in my teaching, the characteristics of spirituality identified here began to emerge as the community developed.

Second, moving to a balance of transmissive, transactional, and transformative teaching approaches and providing students with multimodal opportunities to express their learning not only allows them to engage topics in powerful ways, but gives voice to the spiritual dimension. An example of using a nontraditional teaching mode is showing a slide of the painting entitled *The School of Athens* by Raphael when introducing philosophers, engaging students in a discussion of Greek philosophers through a rich example of visual art. The arts in particular can arouse the imagination of students, assist them in constructing meaning, and facilitate the connection between the inner and outer worlds. Through opportunities to express learning in multiple modes, students are better equipped to engage topics not only cognitively and affectively, but spiritually as well. Examples of this include a group of students who explored adolescent girls' body image through interpretive dance or a student who illustrated a variety of philosophical orientations through the creation of a three-dimensional art installation. Facilitating ways in which students can integrate multiple dimensions of learning provides students with opportunities to express deep understandings in ways in which language fails.

Third, making room for regular silence in the classroom allows both students and teachers to reflect on and contemplate their learning. This, of course, is counter to prevalent approaches which encourage teachers to keep students "busy" so that they do not have opportunities to engage in activities which can be negatively perceived. Silence allows us to reconnect with our inner terrain and our authentic self, which in turn facilitates a deeper level of engagement with concepts, ideas, and each other. For some students it may also be the only period of silence that they encounter in their day.

Fourth, it is nearly impossible to create an open, safe environment for students to explore the spiritual dimension if the teacher is not cognizant of their own spirituality. This requires teachers who are more fully present in the classroom. In most teacher education programs the focus is on theory and practice, and as J. Miller (2007) states, "Teacher presence is often ignored in teacher education despite its importance" (p. 191). If we are to model an interconnected, relational way of being and knowing to students, we must work towards embodying it. In practice this means that we listen deeply to students and that we are present to them. Having presence in the classroom also requires us to develop a practice or discipline such as meditation or yoga that helps us to become more mindful and aware.

Looking at spirituality through this lens, the characteristics of relatedness, interconnectedness, sacredness, transcendence, and connectedness to the earth and the cosmos unfold in relation to one's level of awareness. From this perspective, spirituality can most succinctly be described as a dimension of being. Rather than being externally motivated, it is an internal process or experience which is then manifested through our words and actions, or our interactions with the external world. Spirituality is a deep experience of relationship between inner and outer worlds. J. Miller (2007) defines spirituality as "a sense of the awe and reverence for life that arises from our relatedness to something both wonderful and mysterious" (p. 4). The spiritual dimension is always present, but it is our level of awareness that makes it relevant to us. It is a gift hidden in plain sight.

The development of presence in teacher candidates can be accomplished through embodiment, modeling it for them, and through inviting them to engage in contemplative practices such as meditation or mindfulness training. Chapman and McClendon (2018) describe:

> The teacher must embody what is being taught, with no discrepancy between words and actions, because it is through the integrity of the teacher and the teacher's practices that students develop trust and become willing to take risks, to reveal his or her thoughts, and to experiment with new ideas. (p. 15)

I recommend that teacher education programs be reexamined in an effort to place as much emphasis on helping teacher candidates to develop qualities and dispositions of master teachers as they do on the development of theory, methods, and techniques. Greene and Youngee (2019) support self-development as pedagogy in teacher education:

> There is a critical need to embrace the significant role for personal development in a holistic pedagogy of teacher education. To do so is to acknowledge that we teach—first and foremost—from within. Through a pedagogy of self-development, course curriculum is framed around the centrality of the whole *person* relative to theory, subject knowledge, and skills. This approach invokes the emotional and spiritual nature of who we are as whole human beings. These parts of us traditionally stay carefully tucked away and out of sight, especially in a professional and academic context. (p. 100)

Incorporating spirituality into teacher education as a new pedagogy is not required here; and we are not mandated to teach spirituality, but as R. Miller (2006) asserts, "I would argue that it is the care and love that nourish human development, not the pedagogical ideology" (p. 9). What is called for is an acknowledgment of the spiritual dimension that is already present in all that we do as teachers and learners. Incorporating the spiritual dimension into teacher education programs has the potential to provide both the student body and the professoriate with more holistic, integrative approaches to coming to more fully know and love not only their areas of investigation, but their peers, the world, and themselves.

It is time for the spiritual dimension to be acknowledged in teacher education programs as a means of facilitating integrative learning, which impacts on the formation of future teachers, who after experiencing the spiritual dimension in their academic studies, may choose to incorporate it into their teaching. As teacher educators, if we are to acknowledge the spiritual dimension in our teaching, we must acknowledge and honor our inner lives, gain institutional support, and through embodying wholeness in our classrooms, give our students permission to acknowledge and honor their spirituality as well. This important and ultimately transformative work must begin in the hearts of teachers.

Author Note

A version of this writing was first published in the nonextant journal *Encounter: Education for Meaning and Social Justice,* Volume 23, Number 2 (Summer, 2010).

6

Voice and Choice

Inquiry-Based Learning

Use what talents you possess; the woods would be very silent
if no birds sang there except those that sang best.

—Henry van Dyke

Inquiry-Based Learning

As students connect their inner lives (in the center of the spiral) to their learning, and create relevance, and meaning and purpose (two core features of flourishing), they can then begin the journey outward, connecting with subject matter and peers, and integrating what they have discovered through reflection about themselves and their subject. Inquiry-based learning is one way of providing students with ownership of the learning process and can lead to increased levels of engagement in learning. This in turn cultivates self-determination, which is an additional feature of flourishing. In this chapter I detail an inquiry and peer teaching assignment that my students complete, as well as a description of the development and implementation of an arts camp.

Although inquiry-based learning has been an approach that some teachers have used in their classrooms for decades, more administrators are encouraging (and in some cases, mandating) that their staff implement it in their classrooms when appropriate, as a way to engage learners. There is a spectrum of how the inquiry process unfolds in the classroom. At times it is developed exclusively by the teacher, who selects questions for the inquiry based on specific outcomes from the curriculum. The teacher can also develop an inquiry with the students, which includes more of the students' questions and curiosities. Many students engage in a self-directed inquiry, which is the case in a science fair project, in which the students select a topic related to science, generate a specific question to guide the inquiry, conduct research, and present their findings in a public venue for judges and peers to observe. This form of learning is powerful as it builds on the natural curiosity that learners have, rather than being exclusively directed by the teacher. This is supported by Ryder (2014), "I believe that the ultimate goal of inquiry-based learning is to inspire awe and wonder" (p. 75).

One of the reasons that many teachers are reluctant to use the inquiry process in their classrooms is that they lack personal experience engaging in it and have received inadequate professional development on the process and their role, and as a result they are fearful. As Ryder (2014) emphasizes:

> A common misperception about inquiry is that it is unstructured, it offers the student too much free rein, and it leads to chaotic classrooms. The truth is that it is quite the opposite. Although inquiry-based learning is flexible, as it responds to the interests and curiosities of the learner, inquiry is also structured, thoughtful, and planned. (p. 78)

Some teachers may also perceive that using inquiry in the classroom is chaotic and unpredictable, and Murdoch (2015) speaks to this, "*Inquiry can be messy.* Not in a literal sense (although that too sometimes!) but 'messy' in that, by being more responsive to what students say, do, and reveal, there is less the teacher can tightly control from the outset" (p. 16, emphasis in original). For teachers who perhaps excelled in an education system which was largely prescribed by the teacher, inquiry would be a daunting proposition. In order to understand the inquiry process an educator can engage in research and attend professional development sessions in order to attain adequate information. However, if a teacher has not actually experienced the inquiry process, preparing to adequately implement it with one's students could be enough of an impediment to prevent them from doing so.

It is very rewarding to keep in contact with former students who inspire us, and one of my former students in particular visited my classes for many years with some of his students in the middle years. The purpose of their visit was for his students to teach my students how the inquiry process unfolds in their classroom. One of the things that was an eye opener for me was when they shared how they began their year. The teacher cuts up the learning objectives for a few of the main subjects (typically science and social studies) and gives each subject to a specific group of students. He then tells the students that these are the learning outcomes that they have to learn and asks them if they can think of a project that they could do that would cover most of the learning outcomes. What a brilliant idea! Rather than keeping the learning outcomes hidden, he makes them explicit to his students. One year a group received the specific learning outcomes for a unit on simple machines. They determined that the most optimal way to learn about simple machines was to research, design, and build a trebuchet.

Dave (my former student) then puts their ideas on the board and asks the class if there is a way to create a mega project incorporating the mini projects from each subject. Once again, the students brainstorm and identify a few mega projects. An example of one mega project was the year that they turned their double classroom into a city. Groups of students spent considerable time discussing what kinds of infrastructure and buildings a city needs, and then proceeded to design and fabricate buildings in a variety of zones, including streets and parks. The students worked in groups with each being responsible for a particular aspect and area of the city. They also consulted regularly with the other groups to ensure that there was cohesion in the layout. The result was stunning, as they incorporated green technology into many of the buildings and sustainable practices with rooftop gardens, solar panels, and water features.

Another year, they studied Ancient Egypt and groups of students researched aspects of this civilization that they were most interested in. In the process they created artifacts such as papyrus scrolls, clothing, and a replica of a sarcophagus. This work was set up in a similar fashion to displays in a museum, and they offered tours to other classes in the school over the course of a few days. One of the students dressed like a mummy and rose up from the sarcophagus, which really caught the attention of the visiting students. With Dave's help and supplies donated by parents, the students built a wooden pyramid that was seven feet high in the middle of the room, beside which they fabricated the Nile River with running water flowing through the room. Whenever I visited this classroom the students were busily engaged in learning and were eager to share their projects with me.

Dave often refers to students having voice and choice, and as I have observed his students' interactions with him over the last decade and the quality of their work, I applaud his capacity for risk-taking, and his ability to create such an innovative and engaging learning environment. What was so intriguing about his approach was that the learning outcomes were made explicit and the students had ownership of their learning immediately. In many preservice teacher education programs, the norm is to teach students how to create units and lessons using the learning outcomes, and this is important. I recall creating some very innovative units when I taught early years, and the students definitely engaged in the experiences. However, when students are given an opportunity to make decisions about how they want to learn the mandated curriculum, that is a game changer, for their input gives them ownership of their learning. They usually have much better ideas than we do and there is greater relevance for them due to their input.

It is inspiring for me to observe my university students as these young students in Grades 7 and 8 present to them in such a professional manner. When we debrief during the next class, they usually describe how shocked they were at the students' levels of confidence and love of learning. When we discuss the ways in which the students work with the learning outcomes at the beginning of the year, I usually ask my students, "Why don't all teachers start the year this way? Why do we keep the learning objectives a secret?" These questions of course, point to the results of indoctrination into a particular kind of schooling in which the teacher holds all of the power.

One of the keys to the form of learning that was presented to my students is the sharing of power with the students in the classroom. This requires us to be willing to give up our perceived "control," and to also trust that our students can learn without us leading them every step of the way. Kohn (2011) echoes this:

> Progressive teachers also have to be comfortable with uncertainty, not only to abandon a predictable march toward the "right answer" but to let students play an active role in the quest for meaning that replaces it. That means a willingness to give up some control and let students take some ownership, which requires guts as well as talent. (p. 28)

When teachers control every step of the learning process students can be prevented from deeper learning experiences by following their own lines of inquiry in a manner that works for them. What this requires is for us to trust that students can learn without us controlling them every step of the way. Murdoch (2015) describes, "Inquiry moves the act of teaching out of the realm of control and authority to one of complexity, nuance and some shared responsibility" (p. 16). Educators have varying degrees of being comfortable with engaging this dynamic, based upon their personalities, training, and experience. Some will be very comfortable working with uncertainty and sharing power and responsibility with their students, while others will be pushed out of their comfort zone.

When I introduce my students to unit planning, I now employ this process with them. In small groups I give a few groups the specific learning outcomes for Grade 4 science on the topic of rocks and minerals. I then give other groups the specific learning outcomes for Grade 4 social studies on the geography of Canada. The learning outcomes are cut individually so that the group members can reorganize them as needed. During the following class I ask a science group to join a social studies group and to lay out all of the learning outcomes on their table. Each group takes a turn relaying to the others what the emphasis of their specific learning outcomes is.

I then give each of these amalgamated groups some learning outcomes from Grade 4 English language arts and mathematics. Each group then creates a unit or project that students would complete to learn about all of the learning outcomes. This proves to be highly successful and creates an opportunity for my students to understand how it is possible to take a fragmented curriculum and create a holistic learning experience for their students. Some of my students employ this process when beginning to work on their group unit plan as part of their coursework and they find it very practical.

Another question that I often pose to my students is, "How can we expect students to be excited about learning when we tell them what to do all day long?" This, of course, leads to rich discussion as my students deconstruct their experiences as students and now as preservice teachers. There are specific documents on most provincial education websites detailing how to engage learners, particularly in the middle years. I find this most curious, as the secret to engagement appears to be in plain sight. When we allow students voice and choice whenever possible, more of them will be intrinsically motivated to learn. When students get into senior years and are asked what they want to do after high school and they have no clue, and sometimes they respond with, "I dunno," that is not surprising, as most of them have not had much opportunity to make choices in their schooling. It is crucial that students be supported and guided in making choices, creating a learning plan, following through with their plan, and reflecting on their learning.

The inquiry approach is one way that provides students with ownership of their learning. It gives them freedom of choice regarding their topic and mode of representing their learning, while also having the responsibility for that choice. Most students find relevance in their work as they are driving the process rather than being mandated what to do by the teacher. My initial experience with the inquiry process was when I began teaching in the early years in the late 1980s. Although I was not fully aware of the term or the theory at that point, I was using the inquiry approach. My teaching was based on thematic projects and researching questions that the students posed was a large part of the learning process.

Peer Teaching

Many years ago, a few students in my class were preparing presentations for a student teacher conference that they were going to attend. I asked them if they would like to do a trial run with our class, and they all responded with an enthusiastic, "Yes!" As they were presenting and leading their peers through a variety of activities, I observed the level of expertise and passion that they had, as well as how engaged their peers were. This prompted me to create an assignment for the following year based on the inquiry process. Over the summer I designed the assignment and presented it to my students in the fall semester. My rationale for including it was that in order for my students to fully understand and appreciate the inquiry process, they had to have an experience of engaging it from beginning to end.

The project required them to select a topic relating to education and this resulted in a broad range of themes ranging from nutrition in the classroom to forest schools. The students and I generated a list of potential topics that would provide them with a starting point should they not have a topic in mind. They were to then engage in research and select the mode of representation that was most appropriate for their topic. As they had cooperative discussions once a month in groups of six or seven people, I decided that they would teach the peers in their group. This worked particularly well, as they had worked with these people during the first semester of the year, so group norms and a level of trust had been established.

I determined that self-assessment would be the most appropriate form to use in order to give my students complete ownership over every aspect of the assignment. I recall in one class, when I described the self-assessment, a student asked, "But what are we handing in to you, Lisa?" I responded that they would not be submitting anything to me, at which point several students looked completely stunned and I feared there would be a mass revolt. It was evident that most of them had never done an assignment in which they had total control of the process, including the assessment. I had to gently reassure them to be patient and to trust the process, as most of them had not completed an assignment like this before.

During the next class I asked students in their small groups to make a list of criteria that they deemed appropriate for the assignment and to write them on chart paper. They then posted their criteria at the front of the room and I asked them to identify commonalities. I then wrote these common criteria on the whiteboard and there was consistency from year to year. We then determined a value for each criteria and using a Likert scale for each, this served as their self-assessment.

During the process of creating criteria for the assignment, I had moments of panic, as I had never engaged in this process with a class before. At a later date when I reflected on that experience, I realized that I was afraid. I was fearful that as a large group they would not be able to determine key and valid criteria, which signified to me that I did not trust their abilities. To some degree I also doubted my skills in leading them through the process.

During their peer teaching I observed modes of representation ranging from playing a board game with questions and answers relating to aspects of education; to teaching about countries of the world by preparing and eating food from several countries represented by the student body, including Germany, the Philippines, and France; to doing ice breaker games. It was inspiring to observe the level of confidence and passion that the students who were teaching had, as well as the level of engagement by their peers. I also provided them with questions that I wanted them to respond to after they had an opportunity to reflect on their project and to include it with their self-assessment.

These included:

- Why did you choose the topic?
- How did your research process unfold?
- What did you learn in the process about your topic? About yourself?
- What potential does your topic have to benefit other teachers and students?
- How much time and effort did you put into your assignment?
- Describe your experience of doing an assignment that was totally driven by you.
- Would you use a "choice" assignment with your future students? If so, how? If not, why?

Reviewing their anecdotal responses was very illuminating for me. Many students reported that this was the first assignment they had ever done in public school or university in which they had total control over the process and product. I was stunned. During a discussion regarding the assignment, many students said that they wished that they had an opportunity to engage in a self-directed assignment in early, middle, and senior years. A few students shared that they did have such an opportunity, that they were totally engaged in the process, and that it was the only assignment they remembered doing in school. Some students wrote that they felt overwhelmed at the beginning of the assignment, as the parameters were too open for them, and shared that they had never completed this type of assignment, so had no reference point. I recognized that most of them had experienced 16 years or more of schooling in which they were told exactly what to do and how to do it. Conversely, this was very liberating for other students who jumped at the chance to take full ownership of their learning. Once most of them got into their research and decided how they were going to present their topic, they became energized, as they were following an inquiry into a topic that they were interested in and were driving the process.

Students reported that they discovered that they retain information better when they engage in an activity or assignment of their choice, and most said that being interested in the topic directly influenced the amount of time and effort that they put into the project, leading to feelings of pride in their work. They also shared that because they chose the topic and that it was relevant to them, that they were motivated to research it. Some students researched topics based on a strategy that their cooperating teacher used, some researched topics such as the arts (due to finding a lack of support for them in the school that they had their practicum in), and others chose topics based on specific educational experiences. A few students shared that the assignment allowed them to experience comfort, growth, and learning about a topic that they were interested in, and that it is an experience that they will never forget.

Some students described how they spent more time on that assignment than on any other in their academic year in any of their courses, although the weight of the assignment was only 15%. Upon reflection during the summer and determining that my students gleaned a lot from this assignment on many levels, I shifted the weight of it from 15% to 20% for the coming academic year. When we debriefed on the assignment after the peer teaching concluded, many students shared that because they were assessing their own work, they felt much more relaxed with the process, as they did not have to be concerned about being assessed or judged by the teacher. This was a major insight for them, which I hope will contribute to them implementing this form of assessment into their teaching. As the majority of their responses were very positive and supportive of the inquiry process and peer teaching, it prompted me to continue including it as an assignment, and it has proven to be one of the most valuable assignments in the course.

"Inquiry is really a 'way of being' as a teacher—it is about how you think about learning and the relationship between teaching and learning.

It is about how you see yourself and is at the heart of what you do and why you do it" (Murdoch, 2015, p. 16). I am most comfortable in the classroom when I provide students with concepts and processes and then facilitate ways for them to work with, experiment, and explore this new knowledge, and to then reflect on their learning either individually or collectively. We all know how good it feels when we observe our students having "aha" moments and are reminded why we became teachers. Witnessing my students engage the inquiry process provides me with ample opportunities to observe such transformative experiences.

Voice and choice lie at the heart of education as learners have opportunities to explore topics that are meaningful to them; things that they care deeply about. Through choosing how they want to pursue and represent their learning they develop projects that engage their whole being. The quality of the work that students have submitted based on the inquiry process has been breathtaking, and I have also observed their increased passion for learning. On one occasion a student was interested in the legal and ethical aspects of the teaching profession. She chose to research ethics in practice, the law and code of conduct for teachers in our province, and headlines describing actions that teachers had received suspensions or were fired for. To share her findings, she designed a board game with cards in each of the three chosen categories. For her peer teaching she had her group members play the game. Her peers were totally engaged in the game, and a few days after she presented I asked her if she was going to keep the game. She said that she wasn't sure, so I asked her how she would feel about me keeping it and having my students play it the following year. She was very enthused by this idea, so last year my students played it on two occasions and not only enjoyed it but learned key facts about various facets of the teaching profession.

The Arts Camp

In 2005, my husband Robert Tucker and I were invited by the dean to facilitate an arts camp for children based out of the faculty of education that we worked in. It was an intense learning experience of exploring the application of inquiry-based learning within the context of the arts and was one of the most transformative experiences of my teaching career. This is a detailed description of that teaching and learning experience.

I(nquiry) + A(rts) = T(ransformation):
The Development of an Arts Camp

Imagine going to a place every day for 3 weeks in the summer and being asked, "Where do you want to go today?" This place exists and it provides children and youth living in the inner city with opportunities to discover their world and themselves through exploring the arts. Through following the philosophy and process of inquiry-based learning, engaging the arts, and teaching to the spirit, many of these children and youth ultimately experienced transformation. This is a detailed description of the development of this program since its inception in the Summer of 2005 until the Summer of 2009, highlighting the synergy between the inquiry process and the arts.

This program was developed and operated at a university located in the inner city. The request was to develop an arts program that would answer to the mandate of the university, with part of the institutional mission being to develop working relationships with people that reside in the neighborhood. It is one of the unique features of the Bachelor of Education program. Numerous programs and initiatives have been developed through the years that either offer supports or collaboration with community members.

The arts camp was conceived of by the dean at the time and was supported by the current dean to reflect the focus on community. Community was an essential ingredient in the development of the camp from its inception in 2005, as instructors and program directors met together to discuss what the camp would entail. The dean contacted the two of us, Robert and Lisa Tucker, to be co-directors of the camp, as Robert (referred to as Tucker in this reflection) taught "Curriculum, Instruction, and Assessment of Visual Art in the Early Years" and "Curriculum, Instruction, and Assessment of Visual Art in the Middle Years"; and Lisa taught the "Curriculum, Instruction, and Assessment of Music in the Early Years" and "Curriculum, Instruction, and Assessment of Music in the Middle Years." Based on our collective work over a period of a decade, we were asked on multiple occasions by our teacher candidates to start an alternative school that focused on the arts and had a holistic approach. The arts camp was an example of inquiry-based learning focusing on the arts.

Initial Planning Sessions

Two graduating students that we had both taught, Dave Law and Tanis Westdal, in the after-degree program were selected as lead teachers, and two students from the collegiate associated with the university were chosen as the teaching assistants. At our initial meeting, in which everyone contributed, we decided to offer the camp to children and youth in Grades 3, 4,

5, and 6, who resided in the neighborhood around the university. We were also cognizant of the fact that many of these children and youth were immigrants, refugees, and some affected by war. We began brainstorming the kinds of activities that we could lead with, and as we dug deeper, realized that the only way to make the camp an experience in which students would have ownership of their learning, was to explore the inquiry philosophy and process, and to teach to the spirit.

Based on their work at the Center for Inquiry, Mills and Donnelly (2001) define inquiry as:

> A philosophical stance rather than a set of strategies, activities, or a particular teaching method. As such, inquiry promotes intentional and thoughtful learning for teachers and children. Our classrooms are united philosophically, yet each classroom community is unique because the teachers know it is their right and responsibility to collaborate with children when making the theory their own in their own ways. (p. xviii)

Although we all agreed that the inquiry process would be the most optimal process to use at the camp, we had some reservations. We would describe our mindset as a combination of excitement and fear, as we theoretically believed in the merit of inquiry and had all experienced the joy of learning, but knew that part of our fear stemmed from what felt like diving into the unknown. As teachers and students, we had also had many experiences of learning that were contrived and teacher controlled, with little, if any, opportunity for student input or ownership. We firmly believe that our willingness to step out and take risks and to be in the moment throughout the process contributed to the success of the camp for all involved.

Arts Camp Learning Objectives

We refined the learning objectives of the camp to include the development of an environment for students that would foment

1. community building skills through cooperative social interaction;
2. imagination and creativity;
3. opportunities for self-expression, self -awareness, and self-actualization; and
4. skills development that would manifest personal imagination.

As the learning objectives were solidified, we began structuring the camp knowing that each group of students would have 10 half-day sessions. Students in Grades 3 and 4 attended for the first 2 weeks, and students in

Grades 5 and 6 attended during the next 2 weeks during the month of July. The development of community was deemed by all members of our team to be the primary focus with each group of students, as many of these students did not know each other, the instructors, and were not familiar with the physical environment. Focus classes were also planned in order to provide students with exposure to music, visual art, and drama; to establish a deeper appreciation of each discipline; and to provide a basis for students to discover their talents and preferences for any of the arts. The main body of the classes would be driven by the students' interests with opportunities to work alone, with partners, or in a larger group, depending on the projects that they chose. To celebrate the students' learning, we decided to host a sharing evening in which parents, caregivers, siblings, and other family members would be invited to share the children's accomplishments.

After identifying schools in the surrounding area, we met with the administrators at each school and described the program. This was a unique opportunity for teachers and arts specialists to identify children who they believed would benefit from further experience in the arts in a nontraditional learning environment. The two criteria for student recruitment that we developed were that (a) the student has a need to be creative, and (b) their caregivers are willing to be participants in the process. We were able to recruit 45 participants for our first camp and all involved experienced success.

Many years and approximately 250 students later, as we reflect on the experience of developing the arts camp, we realize that although the instructors and students have changed, the philosophy and approach have remained the same. The following is a sample week. Each of the first few days features a specific art form as a focus, and the remainder of the days are dedicated to the students working on their projects.

The Arts Camp: What We Did

Welcome/Being Together

Although the morning camp began at 9:30 a.m., we began preparing around 8:30 a.m. and our first students arrived around 9:00 a.m. The instructors prepared a sign welcoming the students to the camp, and as the students entered, they were welcomed and directed to the graffiti table where they were invited to draw and talk with each other while others arrived. This proved to be a relaxed, natural activity as all participants had an opportunity to get to know one another while doodling. When all of the students had arrived, they were invited to sit on carpet remnants in a circle and introductions were made, followed by a name game. A variety of cooperative and trust games were played in order to establish a sense of community and to facilitate the children becoming familiar with the space. Snack times were essential, community building times, as breaking bread together is one of the most basic ways that humans gather together, and with the students' input we decided on semi-healthy snacks.

The group then developed guidelines for working together for the next 2 weeks, and they appreciated them not being called "rules." They also made a talking stick with one of the leaders facilitating, and they used it during their regular meeting times. Students were then given paint brushes and paint and a 20-foot long piece of paper and together created a community mural, which then found a home on a wall and remained there for the rest of the camp. The instructors chose the activities based on the learning objectives that we had set out, and we also provided guidance where needed. Some of the activities were gleaned from the work that Tanis and Dave did in the courses that we taught them in visual art and music. The morning typically ended with a sharing time in which campers described how their morning went, where they were at in the process, and if any issues arose, the leaders facilitated a discussion to attempt to resolve the issue.

Students' photos were also taken using a gold gilded picture frame as a prop. These photos were used on either a special sheet of paper for them or in a booklet. Some instructors chose to post sheets for each student with their photo on it on a wall. At the end of each day, the instructors would write something positive that each student had accomplished that day. Other instructors made booklets for the students with their photo on the front and asked students to write what was most significant to them at the end of the day. This constant formative and self-assessment of the students was essential as a contribution to meaningful and temporal feedback for students in developing confidence, identifying their strengths, and guiding them to critical decisions. These formative assessments also became part of a summative assessment at the end of the camp, in which their sheets or booklets were then presented to them during the celebration evening. This process was then repeated with the afternoon group of students.

Drama

Now that the stage had been set, so to speak, students began the day in a similar manner with the graffiti table, then sharing time, and then moved into a focus class on drama. Drama was often selected as the first focus class as it provided opportunities for students to get to know one another and to develop cooperative skills. This typically consisted of warm-ups, trust and cooperative games, and depending on what the instructors selected could

include improvisation, tableaux, and mirror games. These activities facilitated the development of trust and collaboration. The day wrapped up with
a sharing time in which students talked about what they enjoyed during the
day as well as any challenges that they had.

Visual Arts

Instructors often chose visual art as the second focus class, following
the regular morning routine. Tucker taught drawing (up and down lines,
finger painting, and painting to music) to the morning class and then an
instructor would teach it to the afternoon class after watching him model it
for them. For the older students in Grades 5 and 6, one of the most powerful experiences was making masks using papier-mâché. As wet paper was
applied to all parts of the students' faces except for the eyes and the mouth,
the leader of this activity had to be aware and sensitive to students who may
respond with some degree of anxiety. Tucker described the process to the
students and used one of the instructors to demonstrate the process, which
made a positive difference for them, as they could see what the process entailed. Soft music was intentionally played to create a relaxing atmosphere.

Students worked in pairs and Tucker and the instructors observed and
assisted where needed, so that the students felt safe. They carefully applied
the papier maché to their partner's face, stopping regularly and asking
them how they were doing. Tucker also recommended that the person applying the strips of paper talk to the recipient regularly so that they knew
that they were in physical proximity to them.

This activity always felt sacred, as the students were creating an imprint
of their own faces. After they removed the mask and washed their faces, the
masks were left to dry overnight. There was much excitement the following
day, as they returned and looked at their masks. They then painted them
and mounted them on a substrate, which they also painted. These were
mounted on a display wall during the celebration evening and were a very
personal representation of each student.

This mentorship of the instructors by Tucker and Lisa, and the teaching assistants by Tanis and Dave was an integral part of the process, as we
all had opportunities to teach and learn. Some instructors used pieces of
visual art as a focus for discussing the elements of art or the principles of
design. The students experienced a wide range of visual art forms including
finger painting, mask making, making wire sculptures, painting to music,
plasticine pictures, and many more. All visual art pieces that the students

created were kept together with a bulldog clip with the student's name on it, for them to take home at the end of the camp.

Music

The music day would take form again, depending on the instructors' interests, abilities, and student needs. During the 5 years that the camp operated, students experienced a wide range of activities from having Lisa teach them African drumming on water jugs, playing rock-passing games, creating and performing STOMP routines. On one occasion, the dean walked in just as Dave was starting to teach the students the first part of Michael Jackson's Thriller dance. She eagerly joined in and stayed until they had learned the basics. That was impressive! All three focus classes planned for a balance of skills acquisition and self-expression.

Voice and Choice

Day 5 proved to be one of the most powerful days of the arts camp, as students were given the opportunity to begin selecting and planning their projects. The instructors began by asking the students to brainstorm a list of the things that they had done at the camp that they enjoyed the most. These were posted on the board. They then asked them if there was anything else that they wished they could have done, but did not do, and these were included. Our instructors devised a brilliant method for helping the students choose a project without succumbing to peer pressure, by asking them to do a secret ballot. Students spent time on their own, writing down a project (or in some cases, projects) that they wanted to work on and then submitted them to the instructors. As a management strategy, the instructors determined if any students might work together as was the case in students wanting to make a movie. This grouping made the instructors' jobs easier, as they had fewer small groups to work with, although of course, some students wanted to work on their own, which was perfectly fine as well.

A few groups were created for students who wanted to write, act in, and film movies. One group of boys in Grade 4 spent the remainder of the camp creating their own comic strips, which were then enlarged and mounted for exhibition during the celebration evening. Students also worked individually on drawing, painting, acting, dancing, and singing.

We discovered that when students, or anyone really, are given both voice and choice in their work and their lives, that they spend a lot of time and energy working on their projects, because they are connected to themselves and are given freedom to express themselves and their connection with their world. In essence, every day we asked the students to tell us what they wanted to do, and we let them know that we would do whatever it took to help them to get there. When students are committed to the process and engage it authentically, and are given support, it leads to powerful and transformative learning, and as Crowell and Reid-Marr (2013) describe, "When a teacher provides authentic choices she opens up the environment for something creative and original to happen" (p. 37). One of our key observations was that the behavioral issues that did exist during the first few days, were minimized rapidly when students began their own work, which leads one to wonder why more of us do not share our power with our students, and facilitate their learning, development, and fulfilling of their human potential, which is what education is really about.

Crowell and Reid-Marr (2013) note,

> A technical term for choice when speaking of complex adaptive systems is *agency*. There is a "choosing" among multiple possibilities. Process occurs in an environment of choice. It is in the act of choosing that adaptation and transformation happen. This is especially true of human beings. (p. 36)

The students were very excited to have an opportunity to choose their own projects as well as the manner in which they would unfold.

Experience with each of these art forms had a profound effect on the students, as they were gently pushed at times beyond their comfort zones, and some of them recognized that they had an aptitude for a particular art form that they were not previously aware of. Their freedom of expression was refreshing for all of us to witness, as the students were willing to experiment and explore specific aspects of each art form. Greene (1995) states that

> encounters with the arts and activities in the domains of art can nurture the growth of persons who will reach out to one another as they seek clearings in their experience and try to be more ardently in the world. If the significance of the arts for growth and inventiveness and problem solving is recognized at last, a desperate stasis may be overcome and hopes may be raised, the hopes of felt possibility. (p. 132)

As arts education continues to be cut from many schools, including preservice teacher education programs, opportunities for students to learn and express their learning through multiple modes is put at risk. The funding to this arts camp was dramatically cut after the fifth year, which prompted us to not offer it the following year. This can become particularly problematic for an increasing number of students with mental health issues and those who have been traumatized by war and displacement from their homes, as the arts provide them with nontraditional ways in which to express their experiences and emotions.

Performance and Representation

Day 6 to Day 10 were spent working on chosen projects and this is where the excitement began to build. We referred to our approach throughout the camp as "slow learning," as we provided students with the time and space both physically, mentally, emotionally, and spiritually to make room for their dreams to unfold, and as educator John Holt (1989) stated,

> Real learning is a process of discovery and if we want it to happen, we must create the kinds of conditions in which discoveries are made. We know what these are. They include time, leisure, freedom, and lack of pressure. (p. 100)

In a traditional learning environment, one wonders how much time, leisure, freedom, and lack of pressure students experience, and if not, why not?

As the students worked on their creations, their sense of pride in their work was evident. Those who experienced blocks or challenges worked through them and solved their problems, sometimes with our guidance. The intensity with which they engaged their projects was inspiring, and on many occasions, they did not want to take a break for lunch. During this phase of their projects, the large learning space encompassed students painting a large cardboard castle, others working on plasticine pictures, and a group writing a script for a movie. It was a highly charged, creative environment. The students exemplified the power of the creative process as they made deep connections between their inner and outer worlds.

At this point, the role of the instructors and Tucker and I shifted, and we began to do what I referred to as "leading from behind," which entails supporting the students in whatever manner imaginable to help them to become successful. The skills development occurs within the context of the students' projects, which means that the instructors have to know what everyone is working on and where they are at, similar to what a classroom teacher would do when using the inquiry process. The first example of this kind of skills development was when Dave invited a friend to come and work with a group of students who were filming a movie. They wanted to learn stage combat, so Dave's friend brought props and spent half a day working with them, which really paid off in their final film. On another occasion, a few students wanted to create large scale visual art pieces, so Tucker taught them how to draw a grid on a picture that they had drawn, and how to transfer it to a larger grid. Rather than teaching to the whole group, the instruction was imbedded within their projects addressing the specific needs that they had and the problems that they encountered. Mills and Donnelly (2001) speak to the role of the teacher:

> The teacher's role in an inquiry-based classroom remains a paradox. Teachers take responsibility for a leadership role in the classroom, creating curriculum and bringing our own experiences and expertise to the group. At the same time, many teachers try to work themselves into the background so as not to privilege their own voices and to ensure that children's voices are heard and valued above all else. It is not as simple as stepping into the background and letting things happen on their own. It is more about helping children learn to take hold of conversations, to initiate them, and to orchestrate them. (p. 81)

Ryder (2014) echoes this,

> It is not the role of the teacher to be the guardian of knowledge and information, but it is the role of the teacher to guide the inquiry and create opportunities for students to ask, discover, and then ask some more. (p. 79)

Although we had limited time with each group of students at the camp, we were still able to support them in driving their learning experiences. While we thought that we were prepared with adequate supplies, there were many instances of Tucker going in search of large cardboard boxes, fabric, or building materials. During the camp of 2007, a group of students decided to build a castle of approximately 12 feet by 12 feet. Here again a model was created first from a blueprint with Tucker's mentorship, and the campers built the cardboard castle with a working drawbridge and turrets. The students spent days painting stonework on the side of the castle and enlisting other students when they had time to spare. Synergy was created, as this castle was so detailed and lifelike, that another group of students spontaneously decided that they wanted to write and perform a puppet show in the castle. They spent the next week writing a script, creating puppets, rehearsing, and performed their play in the castle on the celebration night.

What was really impressive to us was that some children who were not fully engaged during the focus classes became intensely focused on their commitments to their projects for the duration of the camp. The instructors did an excellent job of guiding and supporting the direction that the children chose through facilitative discussions and collaboration. In observing the children during this part of the process, we were quite struck by their intensity, curiosity, and freedom in expressing themselves. We recognized that an important factor in their high levels of self-expression was the safe and caring environment that was created by the instructors.

As previously mentioned, mentorship was a crucial element of the arts camp and proved to be very powerful in the entire process. We mentored the lead teachers Tanis and Dave, Tanis and Dave mentored the assistant instructors, and both the lead teachers and teaching assistants mentored the arts camp participants. In turn, we were also mentored by all of them. It was a truly collaborative process in every aspect, and everyone benefited from the process.

Teaching to the Spirit

Throughout the process we were all cognizant of what Tucker referred to as "teaching to the spirit." By this, he meant connecting with a person's inner world and honoring and making room for the expression of that inner world. The arts, of course, are naturally conducive to teaching to the spirit, as they are a testament to how humans can express themselves, and we experienced many moments that moved all of us. An example of this was a brother and sister who had come from a reserve to spend the summer in the city. When they arrived at the camp we were not sure if they spoke English for the first few days, but as one of them engaged in visual art and painted nonstop for 5 days, and the other expressed powerfully through drama, they were communicating nonverbally with us in powerful and transformative ways.

Binder (2011) expresses:

> A transformative pedagogy creates a powerful and alternative paradigm for the "what" and "how" we teach, without negating skills or transactional knowing. Through reconceptualizing a transformative curriculum, attention to the innate and spiritual potentials of every child alters the focus of a child-centred classroom to one that is life-centred. (Palmer, 1993 as cited in Binder, 2011, p. 21)

This demonstrated to us that rather than cutting arts programming in schools in order to provide more time for language, mathematics, science, and social studies instruction, that what is really needed is an equal focus on the arts in order to create a balanced curriculum. The participants made deep connections to ideas that were important to them on a personal level, and the result was authentic, creative expression. Edwards (2002) advocates for the integration of the arts in education, "Experiences that enable children to express themselves through the arts nurture their inner life. When children feel a sense of accomplishment and self-confidence through artistic exploration, they experience feelings of personal satisfaction and positive self-image" (p. 3).

Celebration of Learning

The culmination of each camp was a celebration evening, in which parents, caregivers, siblings, and other family members were invited to celebrate the accomplishments of all camp participants. During the last few days of the camp everyone was working at full capacity. All of the artwork was professionally mounted with name tags and titles beside each piece, movies had to be finalized (parts had to be refilmed one year as technical issues erased parts of it), musical routines and puppet shows had to be rehearsed, backdrops finished, and costumes appropriated. We encouraged the students to prepare an introduction of themselves, and to briefly explain what their project consisted of before sharing it. We commenced the evening with a welcome and a slideshow depicting the process that the students went through during the 2 weeks. This not only allowed the audience members to more fully understand what had transpired, but also gave the students opportunities to relive their experience collectively. As product is often the main focus in traditional learning environments (due to having to produce grades for parents and administrators), with the process receiving minimal attention, it was important to us and the students to celebrate the actual process of learning. The students then shared their projects with the audience, food and conversation followed, and finally the students proudly took their work home with them.

Feedback From the Students and Parents/Caregivers

The majority of parents expressed great joy and gratitude for what their children had experienced and accomplished at the arts camp and following are a few comments that the parents provided: "Fabulous!!! It is wonderful that everyone had this opportunity to be themselves." "My son doesn't want to miss a day." "We find ourselves in a real art gallery. Thank you." "My daughter had the time of her life these last 2 weeks. Thank you from the hearts of our family. My daughter had a blast and learned loads which she plans to talk to all her friends about at her new school. Awesome job guys!"

Implications

Our experience facilitating the arts camp was a tremendous experience of personal and collective joy and transformation. The children that attended the camp were our greatest teachers and we feel privileged to have worked with them. We have had many inspiring, skilled, and committed instructors at the arts camp, and we continue to grow in our understanding of the inquiry process by maintaining a connection with them. When asked about the success of this program, it can best be summed up by a group of students in 2009 who realized that they would be too old to participate in the program the following year. On the last day of the camp they all wrote their names and email addresses on a piece of paper requesting to be volunteers the following year.

7

My Journey

May my life flow like a river, ever surprised by its own unfolding.
—John O'Donohue (1999)

The "Spring" movement of Vivaldi's Four Seasons was playing as my students were happily bustling around cleaning up their centers in preparation for our quiet time and dismissal at the end of the day. The mood was joyful. As the students finished their jobs, they gathered together on the carpet, waiting for others to join them. One of my students said, "Miss Ilchyshyn, Brian isn't at the carpet. He's still at his center." I looked over and there was Brian wielding his paintbrush like a maestro, conducting his masterpiece with bold strokes and vivid colors. His body was animated, and he was in the flow. My heart was bursting with joy as I observed this child totally engrossed in his creation, and I quietly replied to the inquiring student that he wasn't ready to join us yet. A few minutes later, he completed his painting, left it to dry on the easel, and quietly joined us for our meeting. That image still holds a lot of power for me, as that student exemplified

Flourishing in the Holistic Classroom, pages 127–141
Copyright © 2021 by Information Age Publishing
127

what engagement in learning was all about, and ultimately encapsulated why I became a teacher.

Moving further from the core of the spiral towards the outer edge, this chapter is a narrative of my journey as an educator, including my experiences teaching in the early years, directing programs and exhibits at a children's museum, and working as an instructor in a faculty of education. This is followed by reflections from former students in the teacher education courses that I teach, describing how they have incorporated holistic principles into their practice.

I resisted becoming a teacher, which was problematic, as both of my parents were teachers, and my sister was near completion of a teacher education program. My love was music and I began playing a toy piano at age three and a real one at age four. My piano was rescued from the beer parlor of the hotel that my aunt and uncle owned in northern Manitoba. I recall the smell of stale beer on it, which my mother attempted to mask by painting it golden yellow, and many of the keys were stained and chipped, but I loved that piano. It was my friend, my therapist, and my voice.

Although music was my first love, and my second was visual art, these were followed by learning of any kind. There was great encouragement and support from both of my parents for learning, and every week I went to the library in the city before my piano lesson and checked out at least a dozen books on topics ranging from dolphins to space travel to archaeology. With the support of my parents, I recall spending hours creating dioramas of zoos, models of houses based on blueprints that I designed, painting birds from stuffed specimens provided by a neighbor who was a science teacher, silk screening Christmas cards, and working on several self-initiated projects for school. This love of learning contributed to my decision to enter the teaching profession.

I was prompted to use my artistic abilities with children as I was a professional musician and a visual artist, spending much of my free time either playing the piano or drawing and doing fiber art. I became quite enthused while working on my Bachelor of Education degree, as I was able to apply my creative abilities in designing innovative lesson plans, unit plans, and other learning activities that drew on and supported the natural curiosity of children. My focus was on literature, as I had been exposed to quality literature as a child, and due to being quite ill, reading became a pastime for me as I convalesced at home. My mother introduced me to the classics (much of it British) with rich settings, imaginative plots, and interesting characters, all enhanced with beautiful illustrations.

At the beginning of my career as an educator, I worked with children in the early years (mainly Grade 2), and it was energizing to work with such curious explorers of their world. Their outward expression of their inner lives manifested through their freedom, imagination, and spontaneity inspired me on a daily basis. Young children are masters of pure *being*, which I believe is one of the reasons that people love *being* with them. They haven't become human *doings* yet but move through their world with great freedom and awareness.

Although I was not aware of the term "holistic education," I instinctively taught holistically, as I wanted children to continue to learn in a way that was natural to them; as close to how they learned before they entered school as possible, thus I incorporated thematic work, the arts, and the project approach. I vividly recall the summer prior to my first teaching job in a Grade 1 classroom, taking the curriculum guides apart and placing learning outcomes into themes that I had selected. I wanted to design learning experiences that enabled my students to make connections between subject areas, themselves, and each other. During our theme on space, I integrated all of the subject areas and we turned our classroom into a spaceship, with plastic strips on the doorway as the students pretended that they were going in and out of it (with accompanying sound effects), keyboards for the control panels, and helmets which each student made. Towards the end of the unit, my teaching partner and I designed a space circuit for students to move through in pairs. Each station focused on a specific activity that an astronaut would engage in, including wearing a welder's helmet and a glove and having to use a wrench to put a nut and bolt together on a large metal stand. As we included a range of activities to address all learners, students thoroughly engaged these activities.

The dinosaur theme was one of the most interesting units that I developed. Once again, I integrated learning outcomes from all subject areas that related to the theme. At the beginning of the theme, students posed their questions about dinosaurs, which I recorded on chart paper. These questions remained on the wall for the duration of the unit and drove much of our inquiry. My students learned all of the learning outcomes from the measurement strand in mathematics during this theme. As a class, we measured the actual size of several dinosaurs in the hallway and marked them. We took the same measurements with dinosaur footprints, drew them to size, and cut them out. I laminated these, which set the stage for the next activity in which students traced their own feet and cut them out. We then determined how many of their footprints fit inside of each dinosaur footprint and my students found this quite fascinating as they pondered the enormous size of these creatures. After this initial learning experience, many students sat in the dinosaur footprints during quiet time or when reading a book.

I turned the sandbox into a "dig" site and created a grid using string. After bleaching some chicken bones, I placed them in the sand at different levels and covered them. As a center activity, students had an opportunity to experience a "dig." With a partner, they used small trowels and dug up as many bones as they could. I created a page with grid lines that reflected those on the sandbox, and students then drew where they found the bones in the sandbox on their paper grid. This provided a level of challenge for some students regarding spatial awareness, yet others completed the activity quite easily. The librarian supplied our class with a wonderful collection of books on dinosaurs, including both fiction and nonfiction. We sang songs and read poems and stories about dinosaurs throughout the month, which supported the students' own writing. As part of the wrap-up of the unit, I guided students through making fossils out of plaster of Paris. The enthusiasm with which my students engaged the entire experience was tremendous.

I taught the entire curriculum thematically, and students were often not aware that they were "learning." As students worked on projects that interested them, I provided mini lessons as needed, so was imbedding the instruction within the context of their explorations. I referred to this as "leading from behind." I later discovered that a lot of what I was doing was inquiry-based teaching and learning. I found this to be a natural process as I fully believed that if I encouraged the children to follow their natural curiosity and to learn through their interests, that I could meet most of the mandated curricular outcomes. It also seemed logical to allow the students to lead with their strengths, and then to use those strengths in developing the areas that they were not as strong in.

I began teaching in the late 1980s when the whole language movement began. The philosophy of whole language was based on children becoming literate through immersion in rich, whole language experiences. I read many books by Frank Smith and others who articulated the philosophy, theory, and practice of whole language beautifully. I attended numerous workshops and at one point was corresponding (writing letters . . . remember those?) with Frank Smith, who became a mentor to me. Children learned to read and write within the context of rich literature, and phonics, spelling, and grammar were embedded within the context of the literature. I also specifically taught spelling, phonics, and grammar, and using this approach, my students flourished as readers and writers.

One year I discovered a beautiful book called *Everybody Needs a Rock* by Byrd Baylor (1974) with illustrations by Peter Parnall. In the book the author described how rocks are special and then provided guidelines for selecting the perfect rock. I read the book to my students and not only were they captivated by the story, but they were interested in the beautiful pen and ink illustrations. After reading the story, I took the children outside and gave them the time they needed to each find a rock that they resonated with. It was a sunny June afternoon with a warm breeze enveloping us, and it was delightful for me to observe my students taking their time finding a rock, picking it up, looking at it, smelling it, feeling it, and deciding if that was the right rock for them. They were totally immersed in the experience. This experience was one way for my students to engage the natural world in the context of their learning. I took them outside whenever possible and worked with the natural cycles of seasons on a regular basis.

When we returned to the classroom each student spent more time observing their rock and writing a description of it, after which they were invited to share their descriptions with the larger group. For the next hour or so they drew their rock, including all of the details that they observed. When they were finished, I gave them each a thin black marker and they traced over the pencil lines with it, creating visuals that were in a style similar to the illustrations in the book. These were then mounted on thick, black construction paper for display. All of my students were engaged in this experience from beginning to end, and many of them reread the book once it was placed back in our library. This experience helped them to develop a more personal connection to the natural world and to their particular rock, which most of them kept on their desk for the remainder of the year.

It was unfortunate that most teachers received inadequate theory, instruction, and support to prepare them to implement the whole language approach in their classrooms. As a result of this, many of them did so poorly, and fewer teachers were using whole language approaches within a decade after implementation (a similar outcome to the open classroom fiasco). At this time, I was invited to join a group of teachers in the school division to develop both a reading and a writing profile, which was a developmental approach to literacy, for students in Grades 1 to 6. This was very exciting work for me as it was an authentic approach to assessing and communicating children's literacy with them and their parents or caregivers.

During my work teaching thematically, I was aware of the unique role of the teacher in this work. In essence, the teacher is a weaver who carefully works with the materials (the students and the curriculum) and is aware of how all of the parts must be woven together in order to create a piece that has integrity and harmony. This is refined work, as we must not only have a firm grasp of all curricular areas, but be aware of our students' individual personalities, capabilities, and life experiences, the dynamics at play with other students, and the curriculum that we are mandated to teach them. This approach to teaching exemplifies interconnectivity and interdependence.

One year I developed a quilt project with my students in Grade 2 at the end of our theme on peace. I began this project by reading them stories about quilts and engaged them in a discussion about their quilts at home. We talked about why quilts were important and some of them made strong personal connections by sharing stories about family members who had sewn their quilts. During one of our story sessions, two educational assistants brought in a few of their quilts and the students snuggled underneath them while I read to them. Relevance was created as a parent brought in her quilt and shared the story of how her grandmother had sewn it and given it to her when she was a child. She pointed out specific squares on the quilt that had a particular story attached to them.

As we had studied the concept of peace for nearly a month, I led the students through a brainstorming session regarding what peace meant to them, and I recorded their responses. During the next class, I gave them each a piece of paper with the outline of a square measuring twelve by twelve inches. I invited them to create an image that represented peace to them, and they worked on their rough drafts for a period in the afternoon. They created images of hands touching the Earth, rainbows, flowers, peace signs, and one student drew a heart-shaped Earth with the word "love" printed near the bottom of the image. After working with each student on refining their images during the next class, I then transferred each image to a piece of cotton fabric.

The next part of the process entailed the students using fabric crayons to color their images. They really enjoyed this part of the process as they could see their image coming to life using the vivid colors. I then permanently set the color by ironing each fabric square. This was followed by the educational assistants and me placing batting under each square and pinning another piece of cotton to the back. The final part of the process was for the students to hand stitch the outlines of their images. I showed them how to hand stitch, which was no easy feat for students in Grade 2, and it was heart-warming to be with 23 students hand stitching for several periods over the course of a few days. There was a relaxed atmosphere created as I played music during these sessions, and the students were very focused on this work. Many of them acquired the skill and the adults in the room assisted students who were experiencing difficulty.

After they were finished with their individual stitching, we put all of the squares on the floor and decided as a group where each one should go based on the design, colors, and sub theme. The squares were categorized using these criteria and through group discussion we agreed upon the overall design, and I recorded these on paper. I then took the squares home and used my sewing machine to attach them together and then sewed them onto a backing for stability. I created a casement at the top of the quilt for the rod to be placed in. When I took the quilt to school, we had a celebration with food and drink, and during a school assembly it was placed on a wall in the common space in the middle of the school.

Binder and Kotsopoulos (2011) support multimodal forms of expression,

> Providing opportunities for children to represent their visual universe through artistic representational experiences, such as drawing, painting, or quiltmaking, confirms Sullivan's (2006) claim that art-making is a form of inquiry that can occur before language and could support the idea of children's visual representations as being graphic thought. (p. 342)

This was a powerful and tangible experience of the collective. As a community we created something that would have been much more difficult to create individually, and through working on the quilt together, we strengthened our community. The children took great pride in what they had created together, and I observed them talking to each other about particular aspects of the quilt when they walked by it during the course of the year. This was a particularly transformative experience for the children and for me.

After experiencing serious illness and being off of work for a brief time in my early 30s, I decided to not return to the public school system, as I wanted to explore alternative forms of education, and shortly after I applied for and was offered a position as director of programs and exhibits at a children's museum. This was a perfect transition for me, and it was a delight to walk through the galleries on a daily basis and observe young children freely exploring the diverse exhibits and learning in a natural, free manner. The museum was an architecturally retrofitted roundhouse in which trains had once been repaired. Naturally, the signature gallery was a diesel locomotive (the 9161) and Pullman passenger car, which offered children opportunities to be the engineman, serve food in the dining car, load the mail bags, and carry luggage on and off of it. It was one of the most visited galleries as children were fascinated with the enormity of the engine, and there were ample opportunities for imaginative play in and around it.

Another popular gallery was "The Tree and Me," which was designed for preschoolers to explore. The tree was an enormous fiberglass creation and provided children with opportunities to enter the trunk and to see beavers above them in water (created of resin). Sounds of birds and other animals filled the gallery and they could climb stairs inside of the tree and go down a long slide on the outside of the tree. There were animal costumes for them to wear for role playing, and a variety of developmentally appropriate, hands-on activities beside the tree.

Observing children learning in a nontraditional learning environment was in stark contrast to the regimented schooling that most children enter at such an early age. Learning is a natural process and children are innately curious and should be supported in their curiosity rather than being made to fit onto a conveyor-belt education system that works best for the adults in charge of it.

One of my main tasks the first year was to redesign all of the existing school programs to link specific curricular outcomes to the museum galleries in order to attract teachers and their students to the museum. The impetus behind this was that teachers had to rationalize their selection of field trips by ensuring that they more closely reflected specific learning outcomes as mandated by the provincial ministry of education. An example was a program for students in Grades 1 and 2 called "Eye Spy." Using a series of beautifully illustrated cards with clues on them, students and teachers became detectives, using observation, comparing, measuring, inferring, and counting skills to find objects in the museum galleries.

I worked closely with the team that created public programs offered on weekends, and they designed innovative programs for families to enjoy together, including activities on New Year's Eve and those associated with travelling exhibits. I enjoyed developing these programs with various teams and they were well received by both students and teachers, thus increasing revenue for the museum. I had opportunities to attend conferences at children's museums in Chicago, Minneapolis, and Indianapolis, and after each trip came back with inspiration to create new exhibits and programs.

I was also in charge of exhibit development and headed up the education team during the development and installation of the "Infrastructure" gallery, which offered children with the opportunity to "drive" a VW bug and operate a miniature front end loader. Booking exhibits for a temporary exhibition hall allowed me to use a limited budget to rent "Color Play," a highly interactive exhibit that invited children to explore the world of color. Those were some of the most exciting times of my career.

Interestingly one of the experiences that I had at the children's museum was pointing to a new direction that I would soon be taking. During my last year there I offered a session for the provincial teacher's professional development day called SAG (Special Area Groups). My session was part of the social studies group, and I gave a short talk about the museum followed by participants engaging in a shortened version of one of the school programs that I had developed. It was a scavenger hunt with each group receiving a backpack with directions and props to aid them in their hunt for specific items in the museum. The number of participants was surprisingly large, and while I was giving my talk, I realized how much I enjoyed working with adults. This was a defining moment for me.

In my positions as an educator and then as the director of programs at the children's museum, I was fortunate to have opportunities to innovate and initiate new programs for children of all ages. It was highly creative and stimulating work. When key internal difficulties in the children's museum occurred, I had an inner prompting to leave my position and leapt without a net yet again. Quite soon after leaving the museum, someone recommended that I apply for a job as a sessional instructor, teaching music methods in a preservice teacher education program. I jumped at the opportunity as I had always found academia enlivening, and while teaching early years I read journal articles and books on a regular basis and attended professional development opportunities whenever possible. I was also enthused at the prospect of combining my love of music and teaching. I was successful in my interview and thus began the phase that I have been in for over 20 years, serving as a faculty member working with preservice teachers.

For the first 10 years working as an instructor, I taught preservice teachers how to incorporate music across the curriculum in the early and middle years. This was extremely rewarding work as I was able to apply my experience as a musician and teacher to this new context. Some students were very excited to have an opportunity to learn how to integrate music into other curricular areas, while others had great apprehension and pleaded with me to not make them sing in class. These courses were only one credit hour each, which was an inadequate amount of time to provide students with experiences to help them to connect with music, learn the language of the discipline, as well as the theory, teaching strategies, and assessment practices.

My main objective in designing the Curriculum, Instruction, and Assessment of Music in the Early Years course was to ease students into connecting or reconnecting with music in their lives on a personal level, and then to introduce them to the elements of music. Classes included musical development, working with instruments, singing with children, and the elements of music (beat and tempo, rhythm, pitch and melody, harmony, dynamics and timbre). I demonstrated how to incorporate music into all subject areas from kindergarten to Grade 4. My approach was gentle as I understood that although some students had extensive musical experience, others were hesitant or reluctant to take the course due to having less than optimal experiences with music in their schooling. I eased them into connecting to music through listening, playing games, and by the end of the nine classes they were playing Orff instruments in ensembles. I also brought in a musician who introduced them to African drumming, and by the end of the session, they were playing a polyrhythm together. This was a powerful example of how music can create community. Many students reported that it was the best class they had ever had in university.

I built on this initial course while designing the Curriculum, Instruction, and Assessment of Music in the Middle Years course. One of the main themes was that of identity and self-expression, as students in the middle years are grappling with who they are and how they fit into society. Building on the work from the previous year, students engaged in larger projects including creating and performing STOMP routines. STOMP is a British musician ensemble who uses everyday objects such as brooms and garbage cans and lids to create polyrhythms. After showing them a STOMP video and doing focused work with them on polyrhythm (the layering of rhythms), students determined themes and storylines in small groups. They had two more classes to develop and rehearse their routines, culminating in a sharing with their peers in the next class. I consistently observed students having a great sense of accomplishment as they worked collaboratively on these projects.

The other large project that they worked on in groups was an inquiry into an aspect of music that they were interested in. The first year that I introduced this assignment to them I became immediately aware that the majority of them had never engaged in an inquiry project. I had to backtrack and provide them with a more solid understanding of the inquiry process to support them in succeeding. The inquiries that they shared with their peers were diverse, including a group who designed and built instruments out of wood, and a group who was interested in music in various religious traditions. This group set out to visit a synagogue, mosque, and Christian church. They created a list of questions which they answered after their visit to each place of worship. In their presentation they shared the results of their inquiry as well as a sample of music from each tradition. Their peers were intrigued with their inquiry and the group members reported that it was a powerful learning experience for them.

During my time as an instructor I have been grateful to my students, as their enthusiasm and curiosity for learning has been heartening, and I have had an opportunity to introduce them to teaching music in the early and middle years, inquiry-based teaching and learning, mindfulness, and other holistic practices. I have always been an idealist, hoping that I could affect change in the education system during my career, and having the privilege of working with preservice teachers made me more confident that positive change would occur. As I reach the 30th year of my career as an educator, I realize that the vision that I hold is far from being manifested. Institutional change is v . . . e . . . r . . . y . . . s . . . l . . . o . . . w. Although institutional change is very slow, I have been inspired and encouraged by the students that I have worked with. Their love of children, enthusiasm for learning, and willingness to try new approaches has been energizing for me. I am confident that the students entrusted to their care and guidance will flourish in their classrooms.

Teachers' Experiences of Incorporating Holistic Principles Into Their Practice

Following are commentaries by former students in answer to the question, "Describe how being introduced to holistic, heart-centered education in Lisa Tucker's course has contributed to your development and practice as an educator."

Claire Burns, Teacher

After taking Lisa Tucker's holistic education course at the University of Winnipeg, I was fortunate enough to have worked alongside her developing curriculum for her course in which we explored nature's effects in the classroom. Before meeting Lisa Tucker, I struggled to allow myself the room to make mistakes. The word "mistake" weighed on me. As an educator, I continuously found myself asking "How could *I* have changed this moment?" or "What did *I* do wrong?" Lisa's heart-centered approach to education enabled me to eradicate this line of thought. She changed my mentality completely by reminding me why I was here and not allowing room for negativity. With Lisa's help, I learned to recognize my present state of mind and to acknowledge my well-being so as to better those around me. Her lessons on mindfulness and compassion have shifted my practice so that I am conscientious of individuals in a classroom first as people and then as learners. This has made all the difference.

Lisa showed me that when we acknowledge those around us as entities who bring an entire lifetime of experience, struggle, emotion, and anxiety to a room, we bring the world to our classroom door. Her work has encouraged me to draw from the wealth of knowledge and culture students bring to a room, and to share the mastery they already possess to create work that is meaningful and personal. Walking into her course at the University of Winnipeg, I was prepared for disappointment in the school system; Lisa's perspective transfixed and transformed me. Her holistic approach to education has helped attune my interests in nature to benefit student behaviours. Lessons on meditation and self-awareness have proved time and time again beneficial to my classes, relieving stress and creating a safe communicative based space for students to exist in. Her approaches take an entire person into consideration, establishing lessons that address all aspects of a person. Since meeting Lisa, I have strived to create the kind of community and acceptance her heart-centered classes encourage. I will continue to develop my own practices with the knowledge she has passed on to me because I have seen firsthand how she transforms students. It is without a doubt that Lisa is an expert in her field and has something to offer every educator.

Scott Durling, Teacher

"You teach who you are" was a front-and-center message I received when first meeting Lisa and taking her course as a student at the University of Winnipeg. The quote, from *The Courage to Teach* (Palmer, 1998b), has been a lesson that has fixed itself to me in the years since meeting Lisa and is one that I draw on often. While in Lisa's class in my third year of the 5-year education program, I was experiencing important changes in my life. I was in a stage of my career where I was grasping at the various strands of what it meant to be an educator, but also, as a young adult I was embarking on making sense of my place and identity in an immense and complex world. Nurtured by Lisa and the ways of thinking she put forward, I came to the realization that my strength as an educator was inextricable to knowing my identity—or as Lisa might put it, my heart.

What emerged over the years since this lesson is that we, educators, are complex—and we work with complex hearts, in a complex system, in a complex world. Our classrooms are filled with children that are exceptionally unique and live remarkably distinct lives. Yet, we attempt to somehow pull the strands of these children's existences together and into our own, all in the attempt to make a cohesive, resilient, and strengthened piece of educational rope that will hold together from September until June. What holds this rope together is how it is weaved and braided so that these strands become interdependent and rely on an experience of closeness and connectedness in order to endure and be successful for those months and beyond.

This process of weaving and braiding students together into connectedness is what I see as the power of holistic and heart-centered education. We must search within and embrace the complexity of ourselves and our students so that the pieces of the whole come together to create an immensely secure and durable entity for learning. What this entity is able to do is be vulnerable in specific areas without breaking: where it's okay to not fully comprehend or know our identity, or how to solve the hypotenuse of a triangle, or what reconciliation in Canada looks like. If we only approached education through one perspective, one direction, without our heart forward and open, and without connection to ourselves and others, we would be going against everything that we have come to understand about the human condition and world. We live in complexity. We are complex. We are meant to connect with each other's ideas, skills, messiness, differences, and similarities. And this is what makes life and learning beautiful.

These lessons are what I experienced and learned with Lisa and her course. For moving forward into understanding my identity and myself as an educator, I began to develop my practice through merging this philosophy with my past experiences. Therefore, one might ask what this looks like in my classroom today? For my grade seven classroom, one way it appears is through two characteristics: time and talking. Outside of regular moments of just being together, each Monday morning I take roughly one and a half hours to have a sharing circle with my students. During this time, we review various topics of discussion, which usually exists as fairly surface-level conversations. Slowly it moves towards the deep and messy discussions that we crave as educators. These surface-dwelling conversations might include items like what students did over the weekend, to what the worst superpower would be, to discussing something that their parents do that drives them crazy. As these conversations become more complex, they result in discussions that revolve around students' observations of their world. For this past year in 2018, it included conversations like analyzing the similarities between the detention of children immigrating to the United States and those who were forced into Canadian residential schools. As one might see, conversations such as these are special and create openness in an environment that sometimes feels constrained. It is remarkable what can happen when you focus on the heart and collectively work at braiding the hearts of individuals together. Not too surprisingly, this was a practice I experienced in Lisa's course and placed it in my educational toolbelt that I use consistently. The result of her work in holistic education and heart-centered learning has been friends, colleagues, and an understanding of myself as an educator and adult in Canada.

Alida Einarson, Teacher

In 2015, I had the privilege of registering for Lisa Tucker's Teaching K–8 class in my third year of university. Lisa Tucker introduced me to holistic and heart-centered education, and I am forever thankful that she did.

This type of education is both impactful for the student and the teacher and has influenced me to be a more mindful teacher in and out of the classroom. Lisa took the time before every class to have a few minutes of silence and when she hit the chime it was time for class to begin. This was how we started each class and it was a way that we were able to clear our heads and be ready for what was to come in the day, and to get our head in the right space forgetting about whatever happened before getting there. Lisa not only told us what holistic education was, but she guided us through it, modeling exactly how it should look in our classrooms, and we are all better for it.

Lisa taught me that the meaning of holistic education is a philosophy that is based on the goal of each person finding their identity and meaning in the classroom, in life, and making connections to all that surrounds them. This teaches students kindness and peace within themselves and allows them to grow into wonderful little humans. Lisa inspired me to bring this into each student I teach to help them be the best version of themselves. After being influenced by Lisa in my third year it was pivotal for me to incorporate holistic education into every classroom I teach making it a strong foundation in my teaching philosophy. I have seen this work wonders for my students and I.

While teaching Grade 1 we started each day with an open heart, and I followed exactly what Lisa did with us. Lisa taught me that learning doesn't mean that a person has memorized a concept, it means that they begin by applying themselves to real world situations and connecting them, which leads to the building of empathy in my students. I did an inquiry-based approach where students guided their own learning. This involved nature walks each day and so much exploration. It taught me that new ideas come from creativity. Creativity is hard for students to express unless they are engaged and able to apply their knowledge in innovative ways. I have taken so much from my time with Lisa, but most importantly following holistic-centered education can allow you to see all your students' individual gifts, and that is the best lesson I have ever been taught.

Dave Law, Teacher

I first met Lisa Tucker as a Bachelor of Education student at the University of Winnipeg. At the time, she was the music teacher for the early-middle years program, and it was the favorite class of most of my cohort—including me. Lisa was kind, authentic, and presented herself as a fellow learner who was fully engaged with her students. You could tell she loved what she did and was as involved in the learning process as we were.

As an instructor, Lisa led me to the idea that learning is an experience of the mind, body, and soul. She asked us to consider the whole child in our teaching, and to create learning experiences that would transcend mere curricula. She taught us to value relationships above all else.

The summer after graduating, Lisa and her husband hired me to be one of two teachers in charge of a summer arts camp for inner-city children Grades 4–6. Lisa gave us complete autonomy to facilitate the drama, art, and music camp however we wanted. With Lisa's guidance, my future teaching partner and I created an experimental, inquiry-based structure to the camp that would become the template for how we would teach for the next decade when we ended up working as teaching partners for an alternative education program.

Lisa helped me to develop my passion for creating a culture in my classroom and in my school where students are an active part of their own education. Lisa continues to strive to foster a classroom where authentic learning occurs and to create an understanding among her students that she is someone who is interested in exploring the truth of our world along with them, and I continue to gain inspiration from her dedication to the craft of teaching.

8

The Invitation

And we've got to get ourselves back to the garden.
—Joni Mitchell

We live in a time of unprecedented change. All systems and institutions are being challenged and some are beginning to be transformed due to the mass awakening of humans who have come to realize that 1% of the population holds half of the wealth on the planet, and that their families' basic needs are being increasingly ignored and denied. The Earth, our home, is speaking loudly through dramatic weather events, pleading with us to work with its intelligence rather than exploiting it for our own use. As Nava (2001) notes:

> Not only science, but also human knowledge as a whole, is undergoing a profound process of transformation. The Newtonian-Cartesian paradigm still dominates the sciences and the everyday view of the world maintained by social groups. Yet a new culture of wisdom has started to emerge, offering a new foundation for observing the planet and the social world in particular.

Flourishing in the Holistic Classroom, pages 143–151
Copyright © 2021 by Information Age Publishing
143

It is expected that just as quantum physics surpassed classical physics and explained the universe more clearly, so too is materialist social science on the verge of being displaced by a science that is holistic in nature. (p. 11)

As I work towards completing this manuscript all people on planet Earth are being forced to change the way they live and work due to the COVID-19 pandemic. The response to this event has been unprecedented in the magnitude of its impact on people throughout the world, as many activities have been curtailed. Most travel has been halted, many people are not working, others are working from home, and the governments of most countries have directed their citizens to physically isolate by staying at home. The education of children and youth has been disrupted, as many of them completed part of their school year in an online learning format. This event has also created an opportunity for many to pause and reflect on their values, priorities, and choices regarding the way in which they live.

What is essentially happening is that we are being forced to rapidly adapt to this situation and to collaborate and innovate on a daily basis as things continue to change. It is a mass disruption of patterns of thinking, feeling, working, living, and being. Systems that were deeply entrenched have been disrupted, and as people begin to realize that many of those systems did not sufficiently support them or their families, they are calling for changes in order to support the creation of a more sustainable and equitable way of living on the Earth.

As some people begin to see the sky for perhaps the first time in their lifetime due to a reduction in air pollution, and to hear birds singing, and see clean water in streams, they are beginning to recognize the extent of their negative impact on the natural world. It is a wake-up call of the highest order and has made us aware of how interconnected and interdependent we are.

This final chapter returns to the outer edge of the spiral, where the movement began at the beginning of the book. It is an invitation to recognize that you are an intrinsic part of the cosmos. As everything in the universe is interconnected, so too, through holistic education, can we create environments in which our students can make connections between themselves, their peers, their world, and their subjects through the entirety of their being.

The emergence of a more holistic paradigm is a hopeful sign, and many positive changes are already occurring including people gathering with their neighbors for times of celebration and support. Local food production has been increasing as is evidenced by a plethora of farmers' markets popping up in cities and towns. Last summer in particular, due to people being mandated to stay home, those who had never done so before planted vegetable gardens. Young people are exploring cohousing and ecovillages as a way to live together more peaceably and sustainably, and there have been a handful of senior cohousing communities developed in Canada within the last decade and others throughout the world, allowing people to age in place and remain in their homes for a longer period of time. People are increasingly using alternative forms of health care including homeopathy, chiropractic, massage therapy, and naturopathy to address their health needs, as many experience allopathic health practitioners predominantly treat their symptoms, while not addressing the root causes of their issues through holistic and integrative approaches.

In 2018, the network of Wellbeing Economy Governments was formed by First Minister of Scotland Nicola Sturgeon, Prime Minister of New Zealand Jacinda Adam, and Prime Minister of Iceland Katrín Jakobsdóttir. They acknowledge that well-being is as important as economic growth and are working collaboratively towards this focus as a way to address some of the most pressing challenges that their countries face.

Indigenous peoples are sought for their deep connection to the Earth, in helping people to cocreate with the natural world, and many of them are instrumental in environmental activism throughout the world. Their cosmologies reflect a deep knowing of the interconnected universe that we inhabit. Nava (2001) states, "The new model is emerging as an integral, ecological paradigm. Its vision of all forms of life on our planet is transdisciplinary and holistic" (p. 11). This model is actually not a new model, but rather an ancient one that is being remembered by many of those who were forced to forget it. For centuries, many societies have had collective amnesia about who we are, where we came from, and how to live in and with the natural environment, which is our home—the Earth. The fragmented scientific worldview was imposed upon the very peoples whose wisdom is now solicited. It is worth noting that many people have only taken note of ancient knowledge and wisdom through scientific validation.

In Hank Wesselman's (2011) book, *The Bowl of Light: Ancestral Wisdom From a Hawaiian Shaman,* he shares the teachings of Hale Kealohalani Makua. Hank and his wife Jill developed a deep friendship with Makua, as he was known, during the last 8 years of his life on the Big Island of Hawaii. Makua was a revered elder and most likely the last kahuna in the islands. Wesselman relayed Makua's thoughts regarding the changes occurring on planet Earth, "The time has come to return to the wisdom of our ancestors, and they are in agreement that we must reconsider these perceived needs." "And," Makua added, "we must begin to produce that which we need at the local level of our communities. In fact, this is about the renewal and the reforming of community" (p. 196).

The wisdom and knowledge of many non-indigenous peoples also offers hope and a way through the devastation that has occurred to our Earth and all living creatures on it, by making others aware of how interconnected all life is. We now have opportunities presented to us, and some being forced on us, which we can use to help us to awaken and remember our organic nature and our role in our ecology. During this climate cycle, we are having to adapt to gyrations of heat and cold in innovative ways including developing new forms of generating energy. It is up to us both individually and collectively to decide whether or not to choose this path.

As education systems are a microcosm of society, changes are also occurring, but often with great resistance. Many people have invested a lot of time, energy, and money in the current system of bureaucratic control and are resistant to considering alternatives. R. Miller (2000) relates,

> The fact remains that education is inherently cultural, and we cannot meaningfully speak about the education of individuals' minds and spirits in isolation from culture or social institutions. We still live in a modern culture that makes the attainment of the holistic vision highly problematic. (p. 85)

Further to this point, R. Miller (2000) states:

> Our educational system, too, is characterized by possessive, competitive individualism. When policymakers and corporate executives speak of "excellence" in education, they are not referring to the refinement of moral and spiritual sensitivity, empathy, compassion, mutual aid or a concern for truth and justice; they are simply referring to young people's ability to compete effectively in the world of selling and growth and bottom lines. (p. 59)

It is time for individual schools to create communities of learners that address the needs, hopes, and vision of their individual contexts, rather than following a structure that has been superimposed upon them. Healthy communities that are responsive and resilient, develop and grow from the inside out, rather than from the outside in. This is reflected in Nava's (2001) work, "From the holistic perspective, above all, it is necessary to transform schools from bureaucratic organizations with a set work routine, into dynamic communities of learning" (p. 117). If we are to provide students with an education that will prepare them for living in an interdependent world, the forms and structures within which they learn must change in order to offer greater levels of support. Berry (1999) states:

Our educational institutions need to see their purpose not as training personnel for exploiting the Earth but as guiding students toward an intimate relationship with the Earth. For it is the planet itself that brings us into being, sustains us in life, and delights us with its wonders. In this context we might consider the intellectual, political, and economic orientations that will enable us to fulfill the historical assignment before us—to establish a more viable way into the future. (p. x)

Crowell (2019) notes:

Teaching for meaning, purpose, and integrated understanding is supported by much of today's traditional research. But holistic education is more than new methodologies, it is a shift in how we view the world. This shift is grounded in consciousness and has implications for personal and societal transformation. It is a creative project that re-enchants not only learning but also the relationship with oneself, one another, nature, and spirit. (p. 295)

Re-enchantment will occur as new structures are created that focus on supporting students and those who work directly with them. Administrators must function more as servant-leaders who support those immediately involved in teaching and learning and in the development of healthy communities of learners. They must be given the power and agency to make decisions locally that respond to the immediate needs of their specific contexts. R. Miller shares,

Maria Montessori said it simply, "Follow the child! *Follow the child.* This is the true beginning of holistic education. An education that starts with standards, with government mandates, with a selection of great books, with lesson plans—in short, with a predetermined "curriculum"—is not holistic, for it loses the living reality of the growing, learning, seeking human being. (p. 69)

In this phase of human and planetary evolution a holistic paradigm has the potential to support us in renewing the Earth, ourselves, and our systems. As human consciousness rises and we begin to not only understand, but to know on a deep level, that everything in the cosmos is interconnected, positive change will occur. Rather than being externally motivated and driven, the connection to our inner terrain as well as to the natural world, will provide the ground upon which we can cultivate compassion. With a grounding in compassion, everything as we know it, including education, has the potential to be transformed.

This holistic, integrative vision will allow us to more closely align ourselves with the processes and cycles of the natural world, thus making us more keenly sensitive to the impacts of our actions on the natural world and all who inhabit it. We will create an environment in which all life can flourish. While technology has partially been responsible for our disconnection from the natural world, it is here to stay, and if used positively, will likely be an important factor in the renewal of the Earth. It is not the tools themselves that are important, but rather the consciousness of the humans using the tools that will either contribute to a rejuvenation of our world or the continued destruction of it.

Wesselman (2011) shares Hawaiian elder Makua's words,

> . . . a new synthesis that must come into being—a conjoining of the tangible and intangible levels of reality that bring science and spirituality together. This synthesis will be brought into being by those working in the field of education and science, theology and psychology, anthropology and philosophy, enabling an extension of our senses and allowing us to access the hidden worlds that lie behind the veil of ignorance and matter. (p. 197)

Educationally, key changes will occur if we view schools as organic structures that are flexible and adaptive rather than assembly lines or sales transactions. Robinson (2009) states,

> For more than three hundred years Western thought has been dominated by the images of industrialism and the scientific method. It's time to change metaphors. We have to move beyond linear, mechanistic metaphors to more organic metaphors of human growth and development. (p. 257)

As communities of trees have highly specialized and sophisticated methods of communicating with and supporting each other (Wohlleben, 2016), so too is the creation of strong communities of learners who care about each other and their learning, important in laying the groundwork for deep learning and student flourishing. The members of the learning community are interconnected, so must create healthy methods of communicating with and supporting each other. Lantieri (2001) affirms:

> I believe we need to see schools as active and alive organisms that place the highest value on self-knowledge, healthy interpersonal relationships, and building community. These goals are not incompatible with the pursuit of academic excellence—indeed, they foster it—but without care, respect, and kindness, what purpose does intellectual competence serve? (p. 9)

Lipton (2005) emphasizes:

> We need to move beyond Darwinian Theory, which stresses the importance of *individuals*, to one that stresses the importance of the *community*. British scientist Timothy Lenton provides evidence that evolution is more depen-

dent on the interaction among species than it is on the interaction of individuals within a species. Evolution becomes a matter of the survival of the fittest *groups* rather than the survival of the fittest individuals. (p. 15)

If learning is solely focused on an acquisition of facts that are at times not relevant to the learner, how can we expect our students to care about the material they are studying? Providing students with regular opportunities to bring their inner self or soul into their learning experiences creates a stronger connection between learner and subject, which in turn lays the foundation for greater levels of purpose and meaning, leading to greater degrees of caring and motivation. Encouraging students to be involved in setting goals for learning and making choices in their topics and the ways in which they represent their learning has the potential to create empowered, motivated learners who have agency in their lives. When students' voices are encouraged and honored, and the teacher shares their power with the students, everyone flourishes. When people know that they have agency in their lives, and that their voices are heard, their attitudes, behaviors, and practices begin to shift in a more positive direction, and they often become more engaged. This in turn, leads to citizens who live their lives with meaning and purpose. We as educators have the power to create this change.

One evening my husband and I were watching a documentary on life in the arctic. He reflected on the time that he lived in Churchill, Manitoba, and said that as he lived in such a remote natural environment, he did not have to take on a mindfulness practice like meditation; just being in the natural environment made him calm and relaxed. This is one of the reasons that we live on an acreage in the country 20 miles from the city. As more people live in cities and have less regular connection to the natural world, they are adopting mindfulness practices to help them to cope with the frenetic pace of their lives.

Introducing mindfulness practices in the classroom is one way to facilitate students connecting with their inner selves. As educators begin engaging in regular mindfulness practice, whether that be meditation, yoga, tai chi, or spending time in nature, we begin to experience an interior change. In essence, this shift makes us more aware of ourselves, as well as our environment and the people within it. As we become more connected to our bodies, we also connect to our hearts and our environment.

The presence that we cultivate through our regular practice can have a transformative effect on what unfolds in our classrooms. In my experience, mindfulness creates a unity and cohesiveness among the members of the classroom, and their interactions become more gentle and genuine. This does not mean that they do not challenge ideas and assumptions, however it is done so with a genuine desire to seek the truth, rather than simply defending individual or collective positions.

Through developing an understanding of the interconnected nature of the universe, and drawing on the natural cycles of our planet and cosmos, we can begin to create communities of learners who flourish in environments that more closely resemble a forest than a factory. Through holistic learning experiences in which the whole person is engaged, students have opportunities to know on a deep level that they not only belong to the natural world, but that they are nature. This grounding will facilitate the cultivation of compassion for themselves, others, and the natural world. From this foundation, the decisions that they make in their education and their lives will have the potential to positively transform our world. I am inspired and heartened by former students who are incorporating aspects of holistic education into their practice, and creating educational environments in which their students clearly flourish.

As we more fully align ourselves with the natural world, and as we become more aware of how interconnected all living things are, we can create the right conditions in which to re-energize an education system that is largely unresponsive to the changes that are occurring at exponential rates. We must once again find ourselves at home in our bodies, our planet, and the cosmos. As Wagamese (2016) shares:

> "Home is a truth you carry inside you." I wrote that a few years back, and I still believe it. Out on the porch, with coffee, a breeze and the calming scent of sacred medicines in my hair, I sit in my truth—this building, this relationship, this day, this certain and assured contact with Creator. I am home. Not just on this street but in this body, on this planet, in this universe. (p. 166)

Teacher education programs hold tremendous power and responsibility to equip teacher candidates not only with theory, techniques, and strategies, but with principles, dispositions, and practices that will prepare them to more readily and confidently respond to many of the challenges they will face in their teaching careers. Although often dismissed as "soft" skills, in the difficult moments in the classroom, they make the difference between a teacher who barely survives and one who thrives. They are the heart of education, and in each of our classrooms we can bring these aspects to all that we do. We can either continue to follow prescribed curricula, policies, and procedures that contribute to the perpetuation of the status quo, or with great courage, we can explore and integrate holistic pedagogy that supports students in not only becoming critical and creative thinkers, collaborators, and innovators, but engaged, confident, and happy human beings.

It is time to create educational environments that more closely resemble an ocean, a symphony, or a forest, rather than a sales transaction or cars on a railway track. As we create these transformative spaces that provide the fertile soil in which our students can flourish, policy makers will have to take notice. As a nautilus shell grows from the inside out, so too will transformation in education begin within the hearts and minds of teachers and students. Wagamese (2016) shares,

> My spiritual father once told me, "Nothing in the universe ever grew from the outside in." I like that. It keeps me grounded. It reminds me to be less concerned with outside answers and more focused on the questions inside. It's the quest for those answers that will lead me to the highest possible version of myself. (p. 23)

What greater aspiration can one have than to become the highest possible version of one's self?

I hope that you may glean inspiration from these writings, and that they may be like wind in your sail, as you navigate the exciting, and at times, challenging waters of teaching. The work that we do, which begins in our own hearts, has the potential to transform the hearts and minds of our students, and ultimately our world.

References

Alderfer, L. (2015). *Teaching from the heart of mindfulness.* Green Writers Press.

Astin, A. W., Astin, H. S., & Lindholm, J. A. (2010). *Cultivating the spirit: How colleges can enhance students' inner lives.* Jossey-Bass.

Bainbridge, R. M. (2000). The spiritual and the intending teacher. *International Journal of Children's Spirituality, 5*(2), 163–175.

Barbezat, D. P., & Bush, M. (2014). *Contemplative practices in higher education.* Jossey-Bass.

Barr, R. B., & Tagg, J. (1995, November/December). From teaching to learning: A new paradigm for undergraduate education. *Change, 27*(6), 12–25.

Baylor, B. (1974). *Everybody needs a rock.* Aladdin Paperbacks.

Berry, T. (1988). *The dream of the earth.* Counterpoint.

Berry, T. (1999). *The great work: Our way into the future.* Three Rivers Press.

Binder, M. J. (2011). I saw the universe and I saw the world: Exploring spiritual literacy with young children in a primary classroom. *International Journal of Children's Spirituality, 16*(1), 19–35.

Binder, M., & Kotsopoulos, S. (2011). Multimodal literacy narratives: Weaving the threads of young children's identity through the arts. *Journal of Research in Childhood Education, 25,* 339–363.

Byrnes, K. (2012). A portrait of contemplative teaching: Embracing wholeness. *Journal of Transformative Education, 10*(1), 22–41.

Caine, R. S. E. (2003). Eco-spirituality. *Encounter: Education for Meaning and Social Justice, 16*(2), 48–51.

Chapman, J., & McClendon, K. (2018). What's love got to do with higher education? How teaching into the heart of knowing can foster compassionate action. *Human Science Perspectives, 2*(1), 9–17.

Flourishing in the Holistic Classroom, pages 153–158

Copyright © 2021 by Information Age Publishing

All rights of reproduction in any form reserved.

Chávez, A. F. (2001). Spirit and nature in everyday life: Reflections of a mestiza in higher education. *New Directions for Students Services, 95*, 69–79.

Chickering, A. W., Dalton, J. D., & Stamm, L. (Eds). (2006). *Encouraging authenticity & spirituality in higher education.* Jossey-Bass.

Cohen, A. (2015). *Becoming fully human within education environments: Inner life, relationship, and learning.* The Write Room Press.

Cornett, C. E. (1999). *The arts as meaning makers: Integrating literature and the arts throughout the curriculum.* Prentice-Hall.

Crowell, S. (2019). Future directions. In J. P. Miller, K. Nigh, M. Binder, B. Novak, & S. Crowell (Eds.), *International handbook of holistic education.* Routledge.

Crowell, S., & Reid-Marr, D. (2013). *Emergent teaching: A path of creativity, significance, and transformation.* Rowman & Littlefield Education.

De Souza, M. (2003). Contemporary influences on the spirituality of young people: Implications for education. *International Journal of Children's Spirituality, 8*(3), 269–279.

De Souza, M., & Watson, J. (2016). Understandings and applications of contemporary spirituality: Analysing the voices. In M. de Souza, J. Bone, & J. Watson (Eds.), *Spirituality across disciplines: Research and practice* (pp. 331–347). Springer International.

Dei, G. J. S. (2000). Rethinking the role of Indigenous knowledges in the academy. *International Journal of Inclusive Education, 4*(2), 111–132.

Dorer, M., Seldin, T., Howe, R., & Caskey, J. (2019). Holism in Montessori. In J. P. Miller, K. Nigh, M. J. Binder, B. Novak, & S. Crowell (Eds.), *International handbook of holistic education* (pp. 161–169). Routledge.

Duff, L. (2003). Spiritual development and education: A contemplative view. *International Journal of Children's Spirituality, 8*(3), 227–237.

Edwards, L. C. (2002). *The creative arts: A process approach for teachers and children.* Prentice-Hall.

Equinox Holistic Alternative School Parent Council. (2021). http://www.equinox school.ca

Fenwick, T. J., English, L. M., & Parsons, J. (2001, Month). *Dimensions of spirituality: A framework for adult educators.* Paper presented at the CASAE-ACÉÉA National Conference.

Finney, S., & Thurgood Sagal, J. (2017). *The way of the teacher: A path for personal growth and professional fulfillment.* Rowman & Littlefield.

Fraser, D. (2004). Secular schools, spirituality and Maori values. *Journal of Moral Education, 33*(1), 87–95.

Gardner, H. (1993). *Multiple intelligences.* Basic Books.

Goleman, D. (1995). *Emotional intelligence.* Bantam Books.

Glasser, W. (1999). *Choice theory: A New psychology of personal freedom.* Harper Perennial.

Greene, M. (1995). *Releasing the imagination: Essays on education, the arts, and social change.* Jossey-Bass.

Greene, W. L., & Younghee, K. M. (2019). Self-development as pedagogy in teacher education. In J. P. Miller, K. Nigh, M. Binder, B. Novak, & S. Crowell (Eds.), *International handbook of holistic education* (pp. 100–107). Routledge.

Greenleaf, R. K. (2003). *The servant-leader within: A transformative path* (H. Beazley, J. Beggs, & L. C. Spears, Eds.). Paulist Press.

Griffith, M. D. (2013). Social networking addiction: Emerging themes and issues. *Journal of Addiction Research and Therapy, 4*(5), 1–2.

Hahn, T. N., & Weare, K. (2017). *Happy teachers change the world: A guide for cultivating mindfulness in education.* Parallax Press.

Hawken, P. (1975). *The magic of findhorn: An eyewitness account.* Harper & Row.

Holt, J. (1989). *Learning all the time.* Addison-Wesley.

Johnson, A. P. (2005, Winter). I am a holistic educator, not a dancing monkey. *Encounter: Education for Meaning and Social Justice, 18*(4), 36–40.

Jung, C. G. (1958). *The collected works of C. G. Jung. Volume II: Psychology and Religion: West and East.* (Eds. Read, Sir H., Fordham, M., & Adler, G.). Pantheon Books, Inc.

Karsenti, T., & Collin, S. (2013). Why are new teachers leaving the profession? Results of a Canada-wide survey. *Education, 3*(3), 141–149.

Kessler, R. (2000). *The soul of education: Helping students find connection, compassion and character at school.* Association for Supervision and Curriculum Development.

Klein, S. R. (2010, Summer). Exploring hope and inner life through journaling. *Encounter: Education for Meaning and Social Justice, 23*(2), 49–52.

Koegel, R. (2003, Summer). The heart of holistic education: A reconstructed dialogue between Ron Miller and Rob Koegel. *Encounter: Education for Meaning and Social Justice, 16*(2), 11–18.

Kohn, A. (2011). *Feel-bad education: And other contrarian essays on children and schooling.* Beacon Press.

Krishnamurti, J. (1977). *Krishnamurti's notebook.* Victor Gollancz.

Lantieria, L. (Ed.). (2001). *Schools with spirit: Nurturing the inner lives of children and teachers.* Beacon Press.

Lindholm, J. (2005a). *Spirituality and the professoriate: A national study of faculty beliefs, attitudes, and behaviors.* University of California at Los Angeles, Higher Education Research Institute.

Lindholm, J. (2005b). *The spiritual life of college students: A national study of college students' search for meaning and purpose.* University of California at Los Angeles, Higher Education Research Institute.

Lipton, B. H. (2005). *The biology of belief: Unleashing the power of consciousness, matter & miracles.* Hay House India.

Love, P., & Talbot, D. (1999, Fall). Defining spiritual development: A missing consideration for student affairs. *NASPA Journal, 37*(1), 361–375.

McGee, M., Nagel, L., & Moore, M. K. (2003). A study of university classroom strategies aimed at increasing spiritual health. *College Student Journal, 37*(4), 583–594.

McTaggart, L. (2008). *The field: The quest for the secret force of the universe.* Harper.

Miller, J. P. (2000). *Education and the soul: Toward a spiritual curriculum.* State University of New York Press.

Miller, J. P. (2007). *The holistic curriculum.* University of Toronto Press.

Miller, J. P. (2010). *Whole child education.* University of Toronto Press.

Miller, J. P. (2014). *The contemplative practitioner: Meditation in education and the workplace.* University of Toronto Press.

Miller, J. P. (2018). *Love and compassion: Exploring their role in education.* University of Toronto Press.

Miller, R. (2000). *Caring for new life: Essays on holistic education.* Foundation for Educational Renewal.

Miller, R. (2001, Winter). Making connections to the world: Some thoughts on holistic curriculum. *Encounter: Education for Meaning and Social Justice, 14*(4), 29–35.

Miller, R. (2006, Summer). Reflecting on spirituality in education. *Encounter: Education for Meaning and Social Justice, 19*(2), 6–9.

Miller, V. W. (2001). Transforming campus life: Conclusions and other questions. In V. W. Miller & M. M. Ryan (Eds.), *Transforming campus life: Reflections on spirituality & religious pluralism* (pp. 299–312). Peter Lang.

Mills, H., & Donnelly, A. (2001). *From the ground up: Creating a culture of inquiry.* Heinemann.

Murdoch, K. (2015). *The power of inquiry: Teaching and learning with curiosity, creativity and purpose in the contemporary classroom.* Seastar Education.

Nash, R. J. (2001). Constructing a spirituality of teaching: A personal perspective. *Journal of Religion & Education*(Spring), 1–20.

Nava, R. G. (2001). *Holistic education: Pedagogy of universal love.* Foundation for Educational Renewal.

Noddings, N. (2003). *Happiness and education.* Cambridge University Press.

O'Donohue, J. (1999). *Eternal echoes: Exploring our yearning to belong.* HarperCollins.

O'Reilley, M. R. (1998). *Radical presence: Teaching as contemplative practice.* Boynton/Cook.

Palmer, P. J. (1983). *The know as we are known: Education as a spiritual journey.* Harper Collins.

Palmer, P. J. (1998a). Evoking the spirit in public education. *Association for Supervision and Curriculum Development, 56*(4), 6–11.

Palmer, P. J. (1998b). *The courage to teach: Exploring the inner landscape of a teacher's life.* Jossey-Bass.

Palmer, P. J. (1999). *The Courage to teach guide for reflection & renewal.* John Wiley & Sons, Inc.

Palmer, P. J. (2003). Teaching with heart and soul: Reflections on spirituality in teacher education. *Journal of Teacher Education, 54*(5), 376–385.

Pink, D. (2009). *A whole new mind: Why right-brainers will rule the future.* Riverhead Books.

Renteria, R. W. (2001). *Teaching as spiritual practice* [Unpublished doctoral dissertation]. The University of North Carolina at Greensboro.

Rogers, G., & Hill, D. (2002). Initial primary teacher education students and spirituality. *International Journal of Children's Spirituality, 7*(3), 273–289.

Rolph, J. (1991). Can there be quality in teacher education without spirituality? *Assessment & Evaluation in Higher Education, 16*(1), 49–55.

Ruiz, R. (2005). *Spiritual dimension in educational leadership* (Unpublished doctoral dissertation]. The University of Texas-Pan American.

Ryder, R. (2014). Cultivating curiosity: Inquiry in the international baccalaureate classroom. In J. P. Miller, M. Irwin, & K. Nigh (Ed.), *Teaching from the thinking heart: The practice of holistic education* (pp. 73–81). Information Age.

Sanguin, B. (2007). *Darwin, divinity, and the dance of the cosmos: An ecological Christianity.* Copper House.

Schiller, S. A. (2014). *Sustaining the writing spirit: Holistic tools for school and home.* Rowman & Littlefield.

Schoeberlein, D., & S. Sheth. (2009). *Mindful teaching and teaching mindfulness: A guide for anyone who teaches anything.* Wisdom.

Schoem, D., Modey, C., & St. John, E. (Eds.). (2017). *Teaching the whole student: Engaged learning with heart, mind and spirit.* Stylus.

Scott, D. K. (1990, Fall). Paradigms lost and regained. *Michigan State University Alumni Magazine,* 16.

Scott, D. K. (2002). General education for an integrative age. *Higher Education Policy, 15*(1), 7–18.

Seligman, M. E. P. (2011). *Flourish: A new understanding of happiness and well-being—and how to achieve them.* Nicholas Brealey.

Shahjahan, R. A. (2005, November-December). Spirituality in the academy: Reclaiming from the margins and evoking a transformative way of knowing the world. *International Journal of Qualitative Studies in Education, 18*(6), 685–711.

Sumner, G. (1983). Synchronicity I [Song]. On Synchronicity. Sony; ATV Music Publishing LLC.

Tacey, D. (2002). Student spirituality and educational authority. *International Journal of Children's Spirituality, 7*(2), 171–182.

Tisdell, E. J. (2003). *Exploring spirituality and culture in adult and higher education.* Jossey-Bass.

Tucker, L. M. (2010, Summer). Quest for wholeness: Spirituality in teacher education. *Encounter: Education for meaning and Social Justice, 23*(2), 11–20.

Tucker, M. E. (1996, April). *Thomas Berry and the new story: An introduction to the work of Thomas Berry.* Paper presented at Harvard.

Turkle, S. (2012, February). *Sherry Turkle: Connected, but alone.* https://www.ted.com/talks/sherry_turkle_alone_together?language=en

Twenge, J. M. (2017, September). Have smartphones destroyed a generation? *The Atlantic Daily.*

University of Hawaii, Hilo. (2019). http://www.uhh.hawaii.edu

Vaughan, F. (2002). What is spiritual intelligence? *Journal of Humanistic Psychology, 42*(16), 16–33.

Wagamese, R. (2016). *Embers: One Objibway's meditations.* Douglas and McIntyre.

Ward, G. (2013). *Spirals: The pattern of existence.* Green Magic.

Ward, G. (2018). The spiral: The eternal sign of the creative and organizing principle at work in the universe. http://geoffjward.medium.com/the-spiral-the-eternal-sign-of-the-creative-and-organising-principle-at-work-in-the-universe

Webster, R. S. (2004). An existential framework of spirituality. *International Journal of Children's Spirituality, 9*(1), 7–19.

Wesselman, H. (2011). *The bowl of light: Ancestral wisdom from a Hawaiian shaman.* Sounds True.

Wilson, S., & Wilson, P. (1998). Relational accountability to all our relations. *Canadian Journal of Native Education, 22*(2), 155–158.

Witts, B. (2009). Seeing the indigo children. *Skeptical Inquirer: The Magazine for Science and Reason, 33*(4).

Wohlleben, P. (2016). *The hidden life of trees: What they feel, how they communicate—Discoveries from a secret world.* Greystone Press.

Yasuno, M. (2004). *Spirituality into action: Exploring the spiritual dimensions of college student activists and their leadership for social change.* ProQuest Dissertations Publishing, 3164335. University of California, Los Angeles.

Zohar, D., & Marshall, E. (2000). *Spiritual intelligence: The ultimate intelligence.* Bloomsbury.

About the Author

As an educator, author, and musician, Lisa Marie Tucker (BEd, MEd) inspires people to connect with their deepest self, others, the Earth, and beyond. She has been involved in holistic education for over 3 decades, serving as a teacher in the early years, the director of Programs and Exhibits at the Manitoba Children's Museum, and for the last 22 years has worked with teacher candidates in the faculty of education at the University of Winnipeg. Lisa is passionate about supporting educators in creating dynamic learning  environments in which they and their students can truly flourish.

For keynote talks, workshops, and consulting, please contact Lisa at www.lisamarietucker.com

Flourishing in the Holistic Classroom, page 159
Copyright © 2021 by Information Age Publishing
159

Manufactured by Amazon.ca
Acheson, AB